HOW TO PREPARE FOR THE BIOLOGY OLYMPIAD AND SCIENCE COMPETITIONS

MARTYNA PETRULYTE & COFFEE

DEDICATION

So I guess you opened this dedication page to find your name. Sorry, mate. Not this time. If only I was an adenine, I would definitely dedicate it to U!

Let me instead dedicate this book to the two most precious XX (nerds…) who won't even read it (they are neither preparing for the olympiad nor are they interested in biology):

1) My most cherished Mom for infecting me with a fatal disease called *life* and

2) My Sister for being my best symbiotic relationship partner.

♥♥♥

CONTENTS

ACKNOWLEDGMENTS

I am grateful to those with whom I have had the pleasure to work on this book. I would especially like to thank Emmy Wang, Sara Cameron, Ayushi Anna Dinesh, and Reneira Seeamber for spending so much time on reviewing the book. In addition, I am especially indebted to my soul mate and best friend Gerta Repeckaite who designed the cover of the book, spent 4 years sitting next to me in school and always supported my biology olympiad goals.

Nobody has been more important to me in the development of my blog Biolympiads.com than Paulius Gedminas, the best computer guru who taught me a lot of extraordinary things.

1 INTRODUCTION

If you love biology and enjoy competing in intense mental fights, or if you just want to torture yourself with endless hours of studying, welcome aboard! The biology olympiad is the right place for you. In fact, the olympiad is something of a paradise (or hell???) for a budding biologist. Don't get me wrong - I'm not trying to deter you from taking part in the olympiads and competitions in the first pages of the book. Hardly! I just want you to be realistic about what you're about to commit to (or already did).

Picture yourself sitting alone in your murky room, studying for weeks, months, years... It's just you and your books. Inseparable like the enzyme and its prosthetic group. Not to mention the fact that you haven't seen your friends or gone to a party in ages. Gloomy, no? Especially when you're a teenager and all these stupid hormones are making you crazy. But... Congrats! Instead of spending your time agonizing over how your life would look if you weren't preparing for the olympiad, you chose a different path. I take my hat off to your boldness, passion and dedication. To learn. To sacrifice. To make a change. And this will change your life. Maybe not today, not the next year. But one day. Don't even try to deny it.

Now let me take a wild guess. You're reading this book because you want to find a divine secret formula which will guarantee your success in the olympiad, or perhaps help you qualify for the International Biology Olympiad (IBO), or at least increase your chances of winning a medal in the nationals. Let's not pussyfoot around this. We both know that thousands of teenagers want the same thing, which is to *win*. So the big question is: How can you outcompete those smart kids? This is hopefully what you'll learn from this book.

Caution! Much of the content in this book is based on my personal and tutoring experience. It reflects what worked for me and where I failed. So chew it slowly like a steak and try out different approaches in your preparation. See what works best for you. Maybe nothing will work. Maybe something will work. I can't give any promises.

Listen, the biology olympiad has completely changed my life. Thanks to all of these competitions I took part in, I met the most amazing people from around the world and visited some of the most unique countries across the globe. Most importantly, the journey towards the olympiad matured me as a person and equipped me with some key skills. What's more, the olympiad is a true 'school of life' which will boost your emotional resilience, and teach you humility and compassion for the self. It'll also show you the price of love and respect. Beyond that, you'll learn how to deal with failures which are really nothing but gifts in disguise. How do I know? See, I screwed up many times. I failed so badly. I disappointed myself, my mentors and others who believed in me. I hated myself for not knowing how to prepare for the olympiad, what to read or what to do in the lab. However, someone once said, "You can't fall if you don't climb. But there's no joy in living your whole life on the ground." And no matter what, I would choose to fall a million times again because everything I experienced during the olympiad journey made me the happiest *Homo sapiens* in the world! Five years later and I still haven't experienced anything like that again… And I probably won't. But you can! And you'll experience it if you put in enough effort. No pressure.

By writing this book, I want to inspire *you* specifically, no matter where in the world you're reading this book. I want to encourage *you* to dedicate your time to biology and the biology olympiad. Hell yes! Everything in this book is there because I believe in *you* and I feel *you* will make the world a better place to live in.

Ready to start?

Let's do this!

Biologically,

Martyna

2 GLOSSARY

You'll soon see that the book you're holding in your hands is full of abbreviations of weird olympiad names. So I put a small glossary below to make your reading journey more enjoyable (and understandable!).

ATP	Adenosine 5'-triphosphate, an energy rich molecule used by the cell.
Campbell Biology or simply Campbell	Campbell Biology textbook is the main textbook used in the biology olympiad preparation.
International Biology Olympiad (IBO)	IBO is a science olympiad for high school students that tests students' understanding of biology.
International Chemistry Olympiad (IChO)	IChO is an annual academic competition for high school students which tests students' understanding of chemistry.
International Mathematical Olympiad (IMO)	IMO is an annual mathematical olympiad for pre-college students, and is the oldest of the International Science Olympiads.
International Physics Olympiad (IPhO)	IPhO is an annual physics competition for high school students.
MCQ	Multiple choice question.

3 ABOUT THE INTERNATIONAL BIOLOGY OLYMPIAD

> **"Certain things catch your eye,**
> **but pursue only those that capture the heart."**
> *Ancient Indian Proverb*

If I may say so, the ultimate dream of every single budding biologist is probably to get to the IBO. In 1990, the first IBO took place in the Czech Republic, where six countries participated. Since then, it takes place annually in a different country. Competition to get one out of the four places in the national team is raising so if you want to qualify for it, you need to understand what it's all about.

Rules

Basically, the IBO is a competition aimed at secondary school students. A national team is usually comprised of no more than four students. The objective of the championship is to bring together the most gifted students interested in biology. There are some strict rules with regards to who can take part in the competition. You have to attend school in the country you're representing and can't have started studying at university. Now, a very important rule is that you can only participate in the IBO *twice*. So if you are in the 9th grade, it's best to focus on building your knowledge and shoot for the IBO in 11th or 12th grade. Although it isn't an official rule, some countries prohibit participation in two or more international competitions at the same time. This means you won't be able to take part in both the IBO and IChO in the same year. However, do check with your national coordinators - maybe your country allows this. Keep in mind that preparing for two international contests is hard work and this can really affect the quality of your studies.

Medal Allocation

What I love about the IBO is that there aren't just three medals (bronze, silver, and gold) in total. In fact, there is a 60% chance that you'll come back with a medal, which is awesome! So how are the medals allocated? The final ranking is based on the t-score method and the medals will be allocated according to the following percentages:

Number of gold medals = 10%

Number of silver medals = 20%

Number of bronze medals = 30%

Also, quite recently, certificates of merit have been awarded to some of the students so the chances of receiving some kind of awards in the IBO has increased even more.

The Exams

The examination is comprised of theory and practical parts, each lasting for 6 hours. Fortunately, there is a day in between the two examinations which allows you to recuperate and recharge your brain batteries. Most importantly, all exam papers are translated into your native language so there is no need for you to perfect your English skills, but I highly recommend it for the social aspect of the olympiad (e.g., for making friends)!

In order to make marking straightforward and quick, all the questions in the theory part (and some in the practical part) are precoded (closed), meaning you won't usually need to provide your own answers (such as writing a small explanation as is required in typical school exams). Another thing is that the IBO questions are usually concise. This means that you can expect more pictures, graphs, pathways, schemes or tables in the questions and less text.

In the practicals, you'll usually get four different experiments to do, each lasting for 1.5 hours. Most likely, you'll get:

A Plant Biology practical, which typically involves preparing cross sections of plants, classifying different plants specimens, identifying different species using a given identification key, or answering theory questions about plant structure and physiology;

A Biochemistry or Molecular Biology practical, where you may have to do an experiment in which you dilute solutions and then calculate concentrations, or it could be to digest a plasmid with restriction enzymes and run a gel electrophoresis experiment;

An Evolution/Ecology/Ethology practical where you analyze the behavior of organisms, and answer questions about ecology or rebuild a phylogenetic tree using given specimens. In this exam, the use of video and/or audio is quite common;

An Animal Anatomy and Physiology practical where you might get tiny invertebrates to dissect. Note that in the IBO, animal dissection is only allowed on invertebrates and fish, or individual vertebrate body parts or organs that are available for human consumption.

Prior to the practical examination, you'll have some time to become acquainted with the specific or unusual equipment that will be used in the examinations. This is quite awesome as your mentors and teachers might have never trained you to use it. Calculators can be used in both the theoretical and practical exams, but you can't bring your own as it'll be provided upon your arrival at the competition site.

The theory part used to be a written exam made up of Part A and Part B. However, since 2013 the exams have usually been delivered on either tablets or computers. The questions test the students' ability to apply general biological concepts and theories, and to analyze and interpret data. They focus more on reasoning, problem solving and understanding, but not on factual recall. Usually, there are around 100 questions in the theoretical exam. If you look at the most recent exam, multiple choice questions (MCQs) are almost completely absent and the majority of exam questions require judging a set of statements on whether each is right (true) or wrong (false). Typically, there will be no overlap between questions and there shouldn't be any questions requiring the correct answer of the previous question.

The IBO's official language is English but all tests can be translated into different languages by chaperones who accompany students to the competition. They are usually post-docs, PhD students or established researchers. Honestly, if you understand English, in the IBO consider doing the exams in English as chaperones are humans too and they do make mistakes which can affect your score (I'm telling you this from my experience with translated versions).

4 MOTIVATION

> *"Believe you can and you're halfway there."*
> *Theodore Roosevelt*

Motivating yourself to study hard is crucial if you want to be successful and achieve your goals in the biology olympiad and beyond. Did you know that if you can master motivation, you can deal with almost any tough situation, as well as inspire yourself to move forward? When it comes to getting results, your strong will and inspiration make things happen. So without further ado, let's get down to business.

Technically speaking, we classify motivation into intrinsic (i.e. self-motivation that arises from yourself) and extrinsic (i.e. a type of motivation that comes from sources outside yourself). It's common that teachers, parents and relatives are the people who spark extrinsic motivation. Let's dig a little deeper. When we are young, we depend so much on others (financially and emotionally, right?). For this very reason, we don't tend to make our own decisions. Others' opinions and influences are so great that when we're 14 or so, we usually don't even ask ourselves what we want and just follow the ideas of those who are around us. You're dead right! Your parents already have a perfect picture of you in their heads. So the only thing you need to do is to make their wishes come true.

However, this isn't that easy. I bet you've noticed that extrinsic motivators are much less effective than intrinsic ones. Have you ever found yourself crawling to the shop to buy something your mom requested while you were playing your favorite video game? Remember how you felt then? Angry? Annoyed? Miffed? Believe it or not, things that others force you to do don't tend to bring happiness. If you really want to be successful, self-motivation is the key. Okey, now you might be asking me where to get that motivation from. How on earth do you become motivated?

I'm afraid there is no one answer to this question. What motivates me might repel you and vice versa. Even so, let me share some things that motivated me when I was your age (and this wasn't thaaat long ago).

1 Find your *why*

Before you start your olympiad journey, outline your goals and reasons for why you want to take part in the biology olympiad. Is it to follow your parents' orders and make them happy? Is it to be the best in your class or school? Is it because you want to have something to boast about to your friends? Or is it because you want to get into the best college and get the highest paying job after graduation? Maybe it's just because you truly love biology and you want to be an expert in the field? Whatever the reason is, you need to know it before you start.

Perhaps unsurprisingly, the reason why I started studying biology in the 9th grade at school was just because I totally, unconditionally, extraordinarily loved biology. Everything from a little crawling earthworm in the garden to a blooming flower to a gross human body and its mysteries fascinated me. Back in the early days, me and my friends built a laboratory in my mom's greenhouse. We brought lots of living animals (for instance, bugs and spiders) from forests there and stocked the shelves up with biology books and microscopes. We even invited our schoolmates to come and see our little Dexter's Laboratory-type greenhouse. The result? My mind became captivated by biology. Another reason was, let's face it, a selfish one. At that time, I was thinking all the knowledge I got in my preparation for the olympiad would help me get into a good university and ultimately enable me to obtain the best possible education.

When you're looking for your *'why'*, think of what the consequences in your life will be if you don't achieve your goal. What will it cost you (I am not referring to financial loss but to social and personal losses)? Similarly, think of what the benefits and rewards will be once you attain your goal. Will your life improve? If yes, how? But why should you ask yourself all these questions? Well, let me first ask you: would you do anything if it didn't increase your academic or personal fitness? After all, life is all about survival of the fittest. So make sure your *'why'* actually makes you more fit in your natural habitat. Just remember that winning a medal in the olympiad shouldn't be a motivator, let alone the goal. Instead, studying biology at the olympiad level should be a springboard to studying this field in much greater depth later in university and to making your contribution to the field.

Bang! You've found your *'why'*. Now, convert it into a dream which you'll always keep in your mind. Next, get a prototype of your dream. I mean, make it tangible, visible, audible, anything to remind you of your dream all the time. Let's say you want to get into the biology olympiad so that it's easier to get into Harvard in the USA (that was my dream) or Oxford in the UK. Write your *'why'* down on paper, make a poster, print it off, stick it on your fridge, etc. Make it reachable - when you can see it, it's easier to achieve it. You can also get a prospectus from your dream university. Put it in your backpack and carry it with you everywhere to remind you of your goal 24/7. And you know what? This will immensely help you get through all those late-night cram sessions and stay-in-and-study days. Try it!

2 Find pleasure in what you do

Let me say this straight - don't do what you don't like. You won't have motivation. And no motivation equals no results. Enjoy every single moment of your life and don't torture yourself. It doesn't matter if you don't qualify for the national round or the IBO. Or even if you don't get into the best university. It's all about the experiences and friends that you make along the way. Frankly, follow your heart and focus on the pleasurable journey, not the destination.

3 Choose to do it

My mom/dad/grandma/grandpa/etc. *told* me to do it. They said I *must/need/have to* read that and study this if I want to go to a prestigious college. Sound familiar? But who likes following orders? Raise your hand if you're keen to do something that is a '*must*'. I guess not many of us will. So my advice is to reframe your language and change '*must*' into '*choose*'. Isn't it more empowering? You're your own boss and *you* decide *what* you want to do, *when* you want to do it and *how long* you will be doing it. Be the one who makes the decision to do something, and forget about the have to's, should do's and must do's.

4 Remind yourself of the feeling

Have you ever won an award? Say, in a dancing competition or in a piano concert? Or perhaps in a sports tournament? Have you ever stood on stage? Have you ever received a handshake and kind words for your achievements from someone important? Do you remember how you felt? What emotions hijacked your brain then? Flick through your memories and remember the feeling you experienced at that moment in your life. Don't you want to relive that moment again? My point is when you retrieve the right emotions from the past at the right time, this will boost your motivation instantly.

5 Track your progress

Another way to get motivated is to track your progress. Draw a small chart like the one shown in **Figure 1**. Jot down who you are now, how much you know, what you like about yourself and what you don't. At the end of the chart, write your ultimate goal. But wait - there is one more thing to do. Dwell on *why* you want to achieve it. Believe it or not, motivation is '*why*' and not '*what*'. Let's imagine you just simply write, "I want to become a doctor." Does this entice you to work harder towards this goal? Well… Not really. All you have to do is to add a little explanation as to why you want to be a doctor. For instance, it could be to alleviate suffering of others, including your loved ones. See the difference? The point is, this will raise your motivation levels much higher because you've got not only the goal, but also an inspiring and even altruistic motive to reach your goal!

Hang the chart in a visible part of the room to remind you about your goal every day. Keep updating it every six months or more often to track your achievements to date. And the best part? This chart will tell you where you stand now, where you're heading, and what steps you still need to take to get to your goal. If you ever find yourself thinking of procrastinating or of any excuses not to study, look at the chart and praise yourself for how much you have achieved so far. Easy, no?

Above all, a lack of motivation can turn you into a monstrous procrastinator. That's when you start to see the real value of being motivated. The simple truth is that motivation enables you to do your work in a timely and efficient manner. Seriously, motivation keeps you focused on your goal and helps you avoid finding excuses! We are all humans and we do give in to the temptation to procrastinate quite often. In the next chapter, I am going to propose some ways that worked for me to avoid procrastination.

Figure 1 Personal Goal Tracking For A Biology Olympiad

5 DEFEAT PROCRASTINATION

> **"What may be done at any time**
> **will be done at no time."**
> *Scottish Proverb*

Okay, here's the problem — we *all* procrastinate. Every single one of us. Every single day. Don't we? It's human nature to put off work and sink into something our souls deeply desire at that time. Something that is relaxing and doesn't require much physical or mental effort. Why? Perhaps the answer lies in the evolution of humans and animals. I hope in biology classes you learned that many animals do mainly three things: eat, sleep, and reproduce. Really, have you ever procrastinated eating food when you were hungry or drinking when you were thirsty? But is reading about genetics of *Drosophila melanogaster* from the biology textbook or doing a Western blot experiment in the lab necessary for your immediate survival? Ahem well no. Doing stuff is energetically expensive, and so if you're not going to die, there's no evolutionary reason to do it. So why would a human use ATP for something outside the remit of survival?

Here's the thing, though.

Humans are typically very competitive. We often 'fight' ferociously to keep one step ahead of our peers whether it's in the classroom or the workplace. We like to show others that we're smarter, richer, or simply better at something. Now, whether your goal is to nail the national biology olympiad or simply to write a good report for a school assignment, your inner angel voice is urging you to do whatever it takes to be the best. But... at the same time, a procrastination devil is whispering in your ears, "See, you're getting good marks anyway. Who needs to study harder when you're at the top of the class?". Such thoughts might become a huge hurdle keeping you away from this goal. What's worse, preparing for the biology olympiad might be super demanding (both physically and psychologically) - you need to read a ton of textbooks, do past papers, and get some basic practical skills in the lab. Oh, and you need to find time for the homework of other subjects, for your hectic social life, and even for extracurricular activities. You name it. When you have a lot of things to do, you'll most likely begin to postpone tasks and almost nothing will be done. This is the point where beating procrastination is a major goal in the biology olympiad journey in its own right. You'll need time to prepare and consequently you won't have the luxury of procrastinating. So what can you do about this? I hope the following tips will help you become more efficient and productive with your time.

1 Set small goals with clear deadlines

I still find myself wondering what went wrong in my preparation for the olympiad. If you're like me, you usually set colossal goals such as "I will read the entire Campbell textbook in 7 days" or "I will review all 20 biochemistry presentations in one day." Gosh, stop now! Such goals aren't realistic. Don't they look so psychologically hard to achieve? When something is tough, long, or in any other way extreme, we'll often find a million excuses to procrastinate. Biology is that field where students are particularly susceptible to contracting procrastination just because it's sooo easy to get overwhelmed by the thickness of biology textbooks and the abundance of revision materials. So how do you become immune?

Set small manageable goals for a short period of time. Get used to setting a small task, accomplishing it, and then move on to the next task. Honestly, such baby steps are my way to combat procrastination and maybe they'll help you, too. As Confucius once said, "It does not matter how slowly you go as long as you do not stop." So instead of reading the whole textbook in one week, it's much more achievable (and easier) to read around five chapters every week. Additionally, the smaller the task, the less stressed out and intimidated you'll be. And a smaller time frame means that you'll be pressed to do everything you can to achieve this small goal on time. Hey, who likes to be a loser who doesn't keep his or her own promises? I bet you aren't one of them.

Now, there are some rules for how to make your goals truly achievable. At university I learnt about S.M.A.R.T goals. Essentially, this strategy makes sure you don't set yourself up for failure by enabling you to define and design realistic goals. S.M.A.R.T goals can be summarized as follows:

Specific   There is a well-defined action you need to take to achieve your goal. It should answer the questions *what*, *why*, and *how*.

Measurable   You have a way to track your progress and evaluate your desired outcome. By gauging your activities, you know whether or not you are making any progress toward your goal.

Attainable	Is it really possible to achieve your goal? Do you have the appropriate knowledge and skills to achieve it?
Realistic	Is your goal realistic and relevant to you? Is it worth your time?
Time-Bound	Your goal is bound by a deadline. This will create a sense of urgency and suppress procrastination.

Let's have a look at one example. A very common goal I hear from many students who want to take part in the olympiad is "I want to memorize the entire Campbell". This goal is specific (memorize a textbook), but not measurable and definitely not time-bound. Also, if you have no set deadlines and measures to gauge success, could it be realistic? Did you think about a strategy or plan for achieving your goal (in other words, is it attainable)? Let's be honest here, if this was your goal, then you're most likely doomed for painful failure. Your goal lacks structure and accountability, and it's simply too ambiguous.

Let's now rephrase your goal to make it a S.M.A.R.T goal. This would sound something along the lines of "My goal is to learn everything from five chapters in Campbell each week and finish all 55 chapters in 11 weeks." Your goal is specific (you want to learn *everything* from Campbell), measurable (you have *55* chapters to learn), time-bound (you have *11* weeks in total), realistic and attainable (you divide your work into *manageable* chunks of five chapters per week so you have a realistic plan that is feasible). What I love about S.M.A.R.T goals is that it helps you measure your progress towards your goal, and this will also motivate you to move forward. So set S.M.A.R.T goals at the beginning of every week. Then, on Sundays review your progress from the last week and set new goals for the following week.

2 Motivate yourself with motivational quotes

As stupid as it may sound, sticking motivational quotes on your walls might help you stay on track and stop procrastinating. Let me ask you one thing. How would you feel if when you wake up every morning or come back from school, you find a quote such as *"It's not about being the best. It's about being better than you were yesterday"* by Unknown staring at you? To me, such words work wonders like a shot of adrenaline to an anaphylactic patient.

Whenever you feel you want to give up, find some good quotes to boost your morale. For example, Winston Churchill has said many heart-touching things about difficulties, fighting and pursuing your dreams. It's a no-brainer to understand that we cease to pursue our dreams once we encounter some difficulties. Don't. Fight every day until you reach what you want. Don't allow mental setbacks stop you. So go and find those quotes that lift you up. That resets your negative mindset. Besides, hang the word *'Impossible'* in your room, too. Don't tell me you never noticed that it actually says "*I'm possible*"? Damn, isn't that so cool?

3 Think about the future

If you're looking for ways to defeat procrastination, try to visualize your future. Simple! All you have to do is tell yourself what you want to get in the end. Think about the achievements that the biology olympiad will bring: The respect you'll get after, the amount of knowledge you'll gain, the best universities you'll be able to apply to and best research internships you'll be invited to join. Think about all the doors that will open to you in the end. And you're set! That's quite a bit of motivation to keep you inspired for some time.

Alternatively, think about who you want to become. Every so often, imagine yourself as an accomplished scientist, surgeon, entrepreneur, or anybody else you want to be. Just don't forget that it's you who will have to do all the hard work to make your way to the very top. So, begin your journey guided by the thought of future *you*. Got it?

4 Reduce the number of distractions

If you've got a goal, that means you need to reduce the time spent on other activities. Just like antibodies are specific for one epitope, you truly need to stick to biology and get rid of unnecessary distractions when you're preparing for the competition. So switch off your computer and phone, find a quiet place to study away from friends and relatives, and inform others that you're now in study mode. Easier said than done, though.

Guess what's your biggest enemy? Ahem, yes! Friends and even family members can actually be a huge distraction, which can slow down your learning process and trigger procrastination. Let's not forget that people that surround you might start blaming you for dedicating too much time to biology and not paying any attention to them. This will cause psychological stress on you which can divert you from your path. So what can you do about it? Ignore them and toughen up your exoskeleton as you will need a lot of willpower to deal with the pressures of your relationships. Mate, if your friends are really compassionate and care about you, they'll understand your commitment to biology without blaming you.

Don't get me wrong - to stay sane, you need distractions once in a while. This is true even in nature. For instance, the intermediate disturbance hypothesis states that species diversity in a particular environment will be greatest at intermediate levels of disturbance. So what's the magic formula to beat procrastination? Plan distractions and incorporate them into your weekly study schedule. This will serve as a very potent motivator which it'll encourage you to work harder. Why? Because you know at the end you'll get your deserved treat.

Keep in mind, however, the value of distractions. Scrolling through your newsfeed on social media or watching videos online may not give you as much satisfaction as hanging out with friends. In essence, commit only to those distractions that make you truly happy and fully satisfied. Then, let those activities set a deadline for your studying. Trust me, it will propel you into focused and efficient work up until your planned (and well-deserved) treat.

5 Use a countdown timer

This is known as the Pomodoro technique, which was developed by Francesco Cirillo in the late 1980s. To me it's by far the most useful tip to defeat procrastination. It's based on using a timer to break down work into manageable intervals which are interrupted by short breaks. So when you're reading a textbook or doing some biology worksheets, set a timer for a specific period of time, say 60 minutes. During that time, do as much as you can of the assignment. Listen attentively to the ticking clock as you're doing your work. Do you feel a rush of adrenaline flowing out of your adrenal medulla!? Feel the heat? Rapid heartbeat? You're now in the excited mode, full of energy and determination to fight or flight for 60 minutes. What I meant is to do as much studying as you can before the timer rings. If that doesn't help when you're studying, imagine that you're in a race. You've got only one shot. Therefore, give everything you can to the task as if it was the only chance for you to show what you can. When the time is up, give yourself a short break (3-5 minutes) and move on to another round of the race.

6 Build habits

Get into the habit of studying for the biology olympiad for at least three hours every day. Just set a study time frame, whether it is from 5pm to 8pm or from 6pm to 9pm. You've got it! Get used to this pattern and you'll soon see that this task is now encoded in your brain as a habit. How lucky you are, friend! You see habits don't need willpower, only repetition. And the habit will make sure you exert consistent daily effort. In fact, consistency, as you might have noticed already, is everything in the preparation of the olympiad.

7 When nothing works, it's time for some pain

Wait, what? Don't be scared - I'm not trying to propose any masochistic techniques here. It won't hurt much. Just a little bit. For your own benefit. Let me tell you the whole story. Motivation usually consists of two P's: **Pain** and **Pleasure**. Above, I emphasized the importance of having some high-quality activities that make you truly happy once in a while. This can be classified as pleasure. And you know what? Pain can sometimes be a good motivator which deters procrastination, too. Think I'm joking?

Naturally, we look to gain pleasure and avoid pain as much as we can. And that's normal as our body is equipped with tons of nociceptors that guard us against any potential injury. But do you remember a moment when you lost a race? Failed a test? Were dumped by your girlfriend or boyfriend? Or were insulted by your best friend (or worst enemy)? Didn't it cause much pain? And then, what did you do in return? Let me guess. You didn't let anger, jealousy, or indifference get the better of you. From that moment onwards you pushed harder to succeed next time. Oddly enough, we *Homo sapiens* tend to tap into the pain inside of us to fuel motivation. Simply put, following some bitter experiences, we'll do everything it takes to avoid going through those experiences again. So where do you get that pain from to boost your motivation and prevent procrastination when preparing for the olympiad?

Don't get me wrong - you don't necessarily need to use some kind of physical pain or torture to keep you away from procrastination. The mere threat of losing something may do the job just as well. Want to see how it works? There are various websites out there where you can set your goals and pledge money towards them. If you veer off the road, you'll be charged whatever you pledged. Alternatively, you can make a deal with a friend. If you fail to achieve a certain goal, you'll lose and have to pay your friend. Try this out and see whether you manage to keep up with your promises. Hold yourself accountable!

6 TIME MANAGEMENT

> *"A man who dares to waste one hour of time*
> *has not discovered the value of life."*
> *Charles Darwin*

Usually, we start preparing for the biology olympiad in 11th grade. I guess it's because this is when we start thinking about our future. Admit it! That's when you're looking for any way to make your curriculum vitae (a.k.a. résumé) and personal statement look good, as applications to universities are looming on the horizon. But hey - it's not your fault. Why the hell would you think about competing in the olympiad? Or about gaining work experience? At your age, these things probably are (and should be) the last on your list. To make matters worse, you have important exams coming up. So how on earth are you going to juggle the olympiad preparation and school work? It'll be hard. But possible.

Let me put this straight. The ideal time to start your preparation for the olympiad is in the 8th grade. You'll have much more free time and most likely no important exams at this stage. However, many of us start the preparation much later. For example, I started mine in the 9th grade, spending the entire year cramming the books and practicing past paper questions. Then in the 10th grade, I took part in my very first olympiad and got gold medals in the school, regional, and national competitions. If you start late, this means that you'll have far less time to do reading and practice the questions. At that point, time management is your only salvation.

Do you often find yourself saying you don't have time to do this or that? That's a common excuse I hear from many people. And it usually goes hand in hand with procrastination. Thankfully, there are some proven (and highly effective!) tactics to help you with time management. Let's get this show on the road.

1 Don't count hours

I receive a ton of emails every day asking how much time one should allocate to prepare for the olympiad. To be perfectly honest with you, such questions really irritate me. When I see anything like *'how much'*, *'how many'*, *'how long'* etc., it just boils my blood. The time doesn't really matter. At all. So don't ask me how many hours per week you should study. I don't know. Believe me, those dreadful numbers will make the entire journey far more difficult, sometimes even unbearable. So forget about how much time you need to spend on reading and solving problems. The simple truth is just get on with your work, take initiative, and just do it. As such, the answer really boils down to "as many as you can muster". Consistently. Focusing on little achievements along the way. And at the end of each day, you'll probably discover that you enjoyed the time spent on biology. On a side note, each and every one of us has different skills and knowledge before we delve into biology, therefore, the amount of time needed to prepare for the contest will vary. After all, the goal isn't to study for a certain numbers of hours but to succeed in the olympiad.

Below, however, you'll find my suggestions on approximately how much time you should allocate to studying. Well… it's for reference only. It doesn't make any difference whether it's three or five hours. It's all about efficiency and how much you can do with the amount of time you've got. So don't focus on numbers, but instead put in as much time as you need to feel comfortable with what you know about biology.

2 Have a plan

Does this advice sound familiar? In school you usually have a timetable and a set curriculum. You have one for your piano classes, one for taking the rubbish out, and so on. You have all these different timetables but you don't have one for the olympiad preparation, do you? What were you thinking all this time? How will you make sure to review all the materials on time? How will you know if your progress is satisfactory if you don't have a plan? These are just a few questions to provoke your neurons to think. Trust me, if you don't have a plan, your preparation may fall by the wayside. Plus you won't see whether you are moving forward or just standing in the same place.

In the section of this book titled 'Study Plan', you'll find some suggestions on how your study plan for a biology olympiad should look like. In our fast-paced world, finding some time to study can be very difficult and thus having a day-to-day plan of what you need to do can help you stay focused. Being organized and knowing what milestones you should reach every day makes it much easier to prepare for the olympiad. Don't forget to leave a buffer-time between your tasks to stay productive. To me, a short break is like a breath of fresh air for the brain. While you're on your break, go for a short walk or run, meditate, eat, call a friend, or do any other mind-clearing exercise that helps you recharge.

In addition to a comprehensive monthly study schedule, make daily plans too. Seriously, one of the worst things you can do is start the day with no clear idea about what you'll be doing. Don't tell me you don't have time to make these daily plans! Jumping from one thing to the next will cost you much more time than the few minutes it takes to plan and think ahead. Make a small to-do list from your monthly study schedule on a post-it note every day, either in the morning or the night before. Get started with the first task immediately and don't postpone what you set out to complete. Knowing exactly what you want to achieve that day and what you need to do will make it much easier to manage your time more effectively.

3 Develop self-discipline

Do you want to prepare for the biology olympiad successfully and learn as much as you possibly can in a short amount of time? Without self-discipline you won't achieve much. Let me walk you through the whole process. By now you should clearly know your overall goals (see section 'Motivation'). But don't just focus on long-term goals like qualifying for the IBO or winning a gold medal in the National Olympiad. More importantly, alter your habits and routines on a daily basis to achieve little goals every single day. Believe me you can be the winner every day. How does that sound? Those small daily victories will have a cumulative effect on your overall motivation. And when you have motivation, you don't tend to waste time on unimportant things. So how do you build your self-discipline?

What do you think about tracking your progress in a journal or a mobile app? I bet this will nurture your accountability. After all, who likes to see their failed or uncompleted tasks on paper? And you won't be able to dispute it. When you see, you care. When you don't see, you don't usually care. Simple as that.

There is another way to foster your self-discipline. Identify role models (for instance, a relative or a friend) who have already achieved the goal you are working towards. Ask them to help you stay on track. Just imagine how much your perseverance will grow if you have another voice encouraging and motivating you and holding you accountable for your progress?

4 Care about your wellbeing

Don't even try to deny the importance of having some ways to relax and forget about studying. Managing your time isn't just about achieving all your goals. It's about being efficient and productive without negative effects at the end. Do you think you'll last long if you just focus on studying? Ignoring physical exercise? Eating junk food? Isolating yourself from friends? No, my dear. Reality is quite different. For maximum performance, eat well to have enough ATP. (Have you ever heard of this joke: "A lad walks into a pub, and asks for a pint of adenosine triphosphate. The waitress says *"That'll be 80p then."*? LOL) Also, exercise regularly to increase blood perfusion in your brain, sleep well to consolidate all that you've learned, and stay positive to reduce stress and increase your endorphin levels.

I made a tremendous mistake when I was preparing for the olympiad. First, I didn't have any structure or plan for my studies. I had a bad mindset as the only thing I was thinking about was how to stuff as much information into my brain as possible. So to reach this goal, I skipped classes at school and instead stayed at home to study biology for endless hours (guess how (in)effective it was?). I didn't have any rest breaks. Not to mention a bad diet and no exercise. Honestly, I ignored many of those above mentioned things. In the end, I was pretty drained although not far from a silver medal in the IBO. So don't take this tip for granted. Make sure you have the energy, physical strength, and stamina to reach your goals. Take it easy and be good to yourself.

5 Be consistent

Here is the problem: we tend to study just before the test, exam, or competition. We are plagued by procrastination until there is only one month or a few weeks left before the olympiad. Why? Well, it's quite obvious - there is plenty of time at the beginning so you think, "I'll start tomorrow." "Or next week." "Or next month." But you never start early enough. Sound familiar?

Leaving just a few weeks for preparation will make you stress out, cram, stay up late, eat junk food, miss exercise, cut out communication with friends, and do all other irrational things. Plus being inconsistent may slow down your progress as your brain cannot handle a lot of information in a short period of time. Do you want this? I doubt it. So how do you go about this? Be consistent. Start early and put in effort every single day. It's of little use to cram multiple hours in one day or one week and then stop studying on other days or weeks. Instead, set aside some studying hours every day. On weekdays, I studied for three to four hours. On weekends, I increased the time to around eight hours a day. When you put in hard work consistently, you'll get results with less effort. All in all, it isn't about squeezing in as many chapters as possible in one day, it's about spreading the workload over time.

6 Learn to say 'no'

We already discussed distractions in the section about procrastination. But here I want to highlight that the skill of being able to say 'no' will propel you forward in your preparation. Too many parties, meetings with friends, or other indulgent activities can easily distract you from your plan. If you say that doing a lot of things can teach us how to juggle our priorities and manage our time better, wake up! It doesn't quite apply to olympiad preparation. If you're doing many things unrelated to biology, trust me, it won't help you much in the competition. So you'd better learn to decline offers and invitations from time to time, and this will help you with your time management. Take on only those commitments that you truly care about. The time you spend on something that gives you pleasure is not wasted time. But what if you're afraid you'll lose your friends if you decline meeting with them? Dream on! Good friends will understand. Bad friends will leave.

7 Be conscientious of time drainers

How many times a day do you check your social media? How long do you spend watching TV or playing games? Browsing social media, gaming, and watching movies are all silent but ferocious drainers of your productivity and time. Don't believe me? Try to track how they're sucking up your time for one day and you'll begin to do them less often. Try to replace such activities with biology-related activities. You've cracked it: do things that create more value for your preparation, rather than things that are mostly empty. For example, when you are commuting, play a quiz game about biology or watch some science-related videos instead of scrolling down your newsfeed. "But what if I can't live without all of these time drainers?" you ask. Not a problem - just include those activities in your study plan. Keep an eye on the time and don't allow yourself to spend more time on them than you initially planned.

8 Utilize weekends

It sounds simple and indeed it is. On weekends, you don't have school and probably any extracurricular activities. This is when you can do a lot of work, read many chapters, and do practice papers. Don't forget to incorporate regular breaks. Hit the library or find a quiet place as parents and friends will be throwing baits at you, trying to distract you from your work. Stay determined. Stay committed. Follow through. With your firm strong will and determination you'll achieve anything.

9 Revise during waiting time

If you find yourself standing in a long queue, sitting in a waiting room, exercising on the elliptical, or waiting for the bus, don't just do nothing. I tended to use that time to flick through my notes or watch videos on the biology topics I was studying at that time. The cool thing is that time flies quickly when you're busy. So a long queue will most likely feel quite short in the end and a lengthy cardio session will end up giving you quite a bit of pleasure (and health benefits!) if you direct your thoughts to, let's say, biology.

10 Start with the hardest, finish with the easiest task

If you want to optimally utilize your time, start with the most mentally demanding task. For instance, reading and understanding a chapter from the textbook. Then, do something that requires less effort, for example, completing practice problems. At the end of the day, when you feel tired but still want to do some studying, do something that requires least effort. For instance, watch biology lectures and tutorials or listen to the audio records. Here's the big idea: focus, attention, and interest tends to decline with time. To put it simply, the longer you study, the less efficient you become. Different tasks demand different levels of thinking, so it makes sense to allow your mind to work hard when it's full of energy and do less when it's running out of ATP. Devoting your efforts to the most demanding tasks first and leaving easy ones for dessert will help you get the most out of your time.

11 Delegate tasks

You can't imagine how lucky I was (and still am) when I was preparing for the olympiad. I've got the most supportive mom and sister in the world. I hope your family is supportive as well because there is always so much they can take off of your plate. Let me give you some examples. Rubbish is piling up, the rooms are getting dusty, the dog needs to be walked, a cake for a school fundraising event needs to be baked, and a painting for art class is as of yet, a blank canvas. Can you estimate how much time all of this takes to complete? Quite a lot, right? When you're preparing for the olympiad, you don't have the luxury of wasting your time on such trivial tasks. So all you have to do is to delegate such unimportant tasks to others. Just don't be selfish. Respect your family and show appreciation. Every day. No matter how hard it sometimes is. You'll realize later how much they helped you and what they sacrificed for you. When the olympiad is over, return your debt with interest to those who helped you when you needed them. No excuses, deal?

7 TEST ANXIETY

> **"Don't be pushed by your problems.**
> **Be led by your dreams."**
> *Ralph Waldo Emerson*

Stress and anxiety are inevitably elements of the biology (and any other) olympiad. Have you ever felt nervous before the competition or when taking the paper? No surprise. It's completely normal! From your experience you know that despite feeling that you're fully prepared to take the test, stress can have a negative effect on your scores. You should have seen me shivering like an eppendorf tube in a vortex mixer before the first biology olympiad I participated in. Then in the exam room, that anxiety hit me like a ton of bricks and I was literally paralyzed in my seat during the entire test. But… handling stress is a skill that you can learn with some practice. Phew! And by knowing how to deal with anxiety, you'll avoid mistakes and do better on tests. Ready?

1 Build confidence

I bet many people have told you to gain confidence in different contexts, no? In the olympiad, confidence is super duper important because when you're confident in your abilities and knowledge, nothing can stop you. Believe me, there is nothing worse than going into the exam and not feeling ready. What's the secret to building confidence? Simple! Work hard. Make sure you are 101% (no, it's not a typo) prepared to sit the biology olympiad test. And when you're in the exam room before the olympiad, ask yourself if you've reviewed all of your notes and handouts, done all your reading, solved past papers, and completed practice problems. Honestly consider whether you dedicated as much time as you could to preparation. Humans are prone to praising themselves for doing little and we usually like to boast about things we actually didn't do. It's crucial at this point to be completely honest with yourself and evaluate whether you did all you could. If your answer is yes, well done! All your stress will fade away and your confidence will probably go through the roof. If your answer is no, well done! Now you'll know how much effort and work to put in next time. In the olympiad (and not only), sometimes we win, sometimes we learn, but we never lose.

2 Get a good night's sleep before the test

You don't need me to tell you how sleep benefits your learning process. Studies show that sleep plays a crucial role in consolidating learned things [1]. In other words, you can keep staying up till really late and stuffing your brain with new information, but you won't learn much this way as your brain won't consolidate what you've memorized. Trust me, this will only leave you exhausted and will increase your anxiety levels in the morning. Aim for no less than eight hours of sleep before the test because good rest will maximize your focus and attention the next day. So a take home message is that sleep is one of your keys to success in the olympiad, got it?

3 Don't revise at all 24 hours before the exam

One thing you should really avoid is cramming for endless hours the night before the exam. Or staying up all night and trying to learn the last few things (see tip #2). It's really tempting to engage in this hard-core brain work the night before the olympiad because you think if you learn something tonight, you'll definitely remember it in the morning. Let me ask you one thing. If you're still determined to revise the night before, which topics are you going to review? Biochemistry? Plants? Animal anatomy and physiology? See, the olympiad isn't like a math test or an English essay. You have no clue what topics will come up so what's the point of reviewing something that may not even be in the exam? It's more likely that you're going to stress yourself out even more (for instance, imagine you realize that you've forgotten to review a particular topic). Or you'll start mixing up all the information in your brain because you just won't have time for making connections in your brain to make sense of the new information. Don't wear yourself out.

Figure 2 46th Lithuanian National Biology Olympiad. Pay Attention To My Table: A Calculator, Pencil Case, And Chocolates!

All in all, don't revise at all the night before the test (at least for 24 hours). No arguments. Period. Instead, go and do something fun like meeting your old friends, calling your lovely grandparents, going for a fancy dinner with your family, or watching a football match. Make sure you come back early to get enough sleep the night before the test. Being well rested with your blood heartily circulating around your tissues is the healthiest way to fight anxiety and stress. And in the morning your mind will be sharp and ready to dredge up everything you've reviewed for the olympiad in the last few months.

4 Fuel your brain

Every biologist knows that the brain survives on glucose and ketones. So in the morning, eat some carbohydrates since your brain loves sugars. Take some chocolates (just avoid any noisy wrapping) with you to the test (look at my table during the olympiad in **Figure 2**). Eat it in the middle of the exam to reset your focus. In addition, tryptophan in chocolate will boost your mood, reduce anxiety and stress.

5 Exercise in the morning

If the exam is in the afternoon, do a morning walk or run to increase your adrenaline levels. This will boost circulation to your brain, wake you up, and equip you with tremendous focus and attention to detail during the test. Moreover, all your stress will diffuse away through your sweat glands. FYI, this exercise does not have to be anything long or exhausting. Fifteen to twenty minutes will do the trick. Don't you dare skip this tip!

6 Turn up to the test early

Leave yourself plenty of time to arrive on time at the venue where the olympiad will take place. You definitely don't want to aggravate your anxiety by stressing out that you'll be late for the exam, do you? It's always better to be early than sorry.

Pack pens, pencils, a calculator, a ruler, and your sweets the night before. Set the alarm clock and ask your parents to wake you up as well just in case. Get up at least two hours before the exam. Take a soothing shower first thing in the morning to wake you up and help you flush out all that stress. Prepare calmly and don't rush as this will trigger the release of adrenaline.

7 Talk with people in the room

Don't be the leave-me-alone type when you arrive at the venue. Go and socialize with people even though you don't know them (I did and met the most amazing people on the Earth). Ask them how they feel, whether it's their first time in the olympiad, and what questions or topics they are expecting to see in the test. Be positive and encourage them. Remember that your positive thinking will reduce your anxiety.

Warning! Stay away from those freaks who are revising from their notes and are frantically trying to memorize what they failed to learn. They will do nothing for your stress levels and can even aggravate your mental state. Remember that stress is contagious so stay away from those who show any symptoms of anxiety or irrational behavior.

8 Use earplugs

To me there is nothing as disturbing and stressful as hearing everyone else in the room scribbling away, turning pages, and making any kind of weird noises. Can you imagine that in this beautiful world there are nasty people who intentionally make loud noises during the test to disturb others (yes, I met such people in regionals and nationals)? Whatever! Just plug your ears using some good soundproof earplugs and pay attention to your own test. Forget about the others in the room. It's just you and your paper. This will help keep you stress-free and concentrated on the exam itself.

9 Have your wristwatch in front of you on the table

Being quick and finishing the test on time is crucial if you want to succeed. During all of my olympiads, I used to take my wristwatch off and put it in front of me. Why? It really helped me pace myself. Plus, being time-conscious will help you reduce your stress as you know for sure how much time you've got left. I would always allocate 75% of my time to look at the whole paper and leave the other 25% to review the answers and check for mistakes. So if you have two hours for the exam, allocate 1.5 hours to do the whole paper and leave 30 minutes for review.

10 Don't cheat. Ever.

Many students feel anxious and stressed out before the test because they're trying to cheat. If you have any small notes hidden in your wristwatch or in your pocket, get rid of them ASAP. There is nothing worse than winning something you didn't deserve. Be honest with yourself. Most importantly, be bold enough to acknowledge that this time you aren't as ready for the olympiad as you would like to be. Hey, there is nothing wrong with this! It just means that next time you'll have to work harder to achieve what you want. Listen to these mind-blowing words of Sophocles: "I would prefer even to fail with honor than win by cheating." Believe me, cheating won't take you far in the biology olympiad (and in any other situation in life). And in the end, what would you put on your cheat sheet? Biology is simply too broad so it's impossible to predict what will come up in the test.

11 Ditch negative thoughts

Eliminate negative thoughts and self-hating statements such as "I'm gonna fail because I'm so stupid" from your mind. This constant negative thinking and self-hatred may lower your confidence and limit your ability to perform well on the biology olympiad test. Oh, and it won't help you manage your stress either, mate. Replace these negative thoughts with some honest positive statements like, "I've been studying hard for X amount of months and I should do quite well on this test." Thinking in this way will bolster your sense of confidence and respect. In addition, positive attitude will keep you anxiety-free.

12 Evaluate the overall value of the test

Okey, you might still be anxious after reading all of these little tips. Now, put the olympiad paper you're about to take into perspective. Calculate its value in terms of your life and your future career. Does it really matter that much to you? More than your health? Your family? Your little doggy? Probably, no. The biology olympiad is a game. You'll either learn (remember in olympiads we don't use the word 'lose') or win, but it won't change anything much. Play fairly and with passion. Remind yourself how much time and effort you put into the preparation. Show everyone your hard work, intelligence, and knowledge! Enjoy those few hours of the game, because it's much more interesting to fight for something you love than to live for nothing, right?

13 Appreciate the opportunity

Feel the power of the paper and look at it as if it was the door to the bigger world, outside of your classroom, town, or country. Appreciate this once-in-a-lifetime opportunity to be able to sit the test. There are so many teenagers out there who would love to be in your shoes. Don't let them down, friend. Show them your best. Get the following words of Blaise Pascal into your head - "It is the fight alone that pleases us, not the victory."

14 Listen to music you like

Before the exam, listen to music that you adore. I bet you know how relaxing this is. What's more, it may elevate your mood and boost your endorphin levels. Many say that classical music is the best choice but find something that activates your neurons. Perhaps it's jazz or hard rock. For me it was Spanish pop music.

15 Let it all out

If you feel stressed out, don't hold it in. Find someone who will listen to you. Scream from the top of your lungs and let it all out. Seriously, this will take some of the burden of stress off of your shoulders. Piling up all your anxiety inside may be harmful as we, unlike plants, don't have the cell walls that would prevent us from bursting open. So free yourself from stressful thoughts and insecurities.

8 LEARNING STYLES

"Tell me and I forget.
Teach me and I remember.
Involve me and I learn."
Benjamin Franklin

Have you ever heard of different learning styles? Probably a million times. But have you ever tried to use them to accelerate your learning journey? Honestly, I didn't know anything about different learning techniques until I got into the university. See, evidence-based learning strategies can be a huge help when you're preparing for the biology olympiad because they are there to help make your studying quicker and more effective.

So far, many different theories have been proposed with regards to different types of learning and over 70 different learning style schemes have been identified [2]. To keep things simple, let's just focus on the three most popular types: Kinesthetic, visual, and auditory. I bet you've got a particular way of studying and it's probably very different from your classmates' way of learning. Let's dig into some facts about learning styles, which may help you understand how you learn.

Figure 3 Doing A Biochemistry Practical To Gain Essential Lab Skills

Kinesthetic learning

Kinesthetic learners absorb new information and facts through hands-on activities. Typical lessons will probably be of no benefit to you. Instead, practicals in the lab (**Figure 3**) and hands-on tutorials are crucial for your success. While studying, you need to use all of your senses and motor functions — the more of this you do, the better you'll remember a particular concept. One very common way kinesthetic learners memorize information is by writing a ton of notes. But hey, what's the point of those notes if you don't review them regularly? I can tell you with a p value less than 0.05 that you need to go over your notes again and again, and then to create a new, more concise set of notes as time goes by (if you want to learn how to create notes, check out the section titled 'Note Taking Techniques' where you'll find a bunch of tips).

This learning style is actually my preferred style. More specifically, I am a read/write learner. As you can guess from the name, I learn best by reading once and writing the same concept on a piece of paper millions of times. Yes, I am exaggerating a bit here. In reality, I write the concept about 20 times in one go and it stays in my head for a long time. Perhaps it's because I use a combination of the motor and visual functions to get information into my head.

Visual learning

If you are a visual learner, you'll learn best through seeing things like graphs, diagrams, flow charts, and pictures. When reading a biology textbook at home, try developing a system of symbols and icons to substitute for the written words. For example, instead of writing out certain biological terms like 'the sun', 'the leaf', or 'the lungs', draw miniature symbols to represent these words. Also, instead of 'increase' or 'decrease', use the symbols ↑ and ↓. Instead of words like 'causes' or 'leads to', write →. Use smiley or sad faces when you are taking notes about something like different types of symbiosis or about a particular experiment that had a positive and negative outcome. Visual learners usually remember pictures instead of words so replace as many words as you can with illustrations. Isn't remembering a picture much easier than trying to recall the word itself!? Another useful trick is to take your notes in a landscape format instead of on a portrait A4 page. This way you'll have more space to include diagrams, flow charts etc. Use a color code in your notes in order to easily spot key details during revision.

Auditory learning

Do you like listening to lectures, podcasts, or videos? Then your diagnosis is that you're an auditory learner. Changes in the advancement and use of technology in education has already helped many teenagers like you with the auditory learning style. Watching videos can double the effectiveness of your studying since you are combining both visual and auditory outputs (remember, the more senses you use, the better you'll remember). What's more amazing - you can listen to some geeky audios on the go, anytime, anywhere. For example, when you are exercising, walking to school or showering. Plus, you don't need to use your eyes to do the hard work. But here's one little caveat - multitasking might decrease your focus on the actual recording and it might affect the quality of your studying. So maybe it's better to focus 100% on listening if you are trying to grasp a very complex topic and mix listening with doing something else when you are just revising. Try and see what works best for you. Furthermore, attending group discussions, lectures, tutoring classes and any scientific events is crucial for auditory learners. Your school may have some science clubs so check them out. Studying in a group is much better as you can listen to others and share your knowledge.

Although plenty has been written about learning styles, evidence is still lacking to show the link between students' preferred learning style and performance [3]. So while scientists are trying to identify and describe the different types of learning styles, take into account your interest in the study topic and try out different ways of learning. What's more, plastic is fantastic when it comes to neurobiology (OK, if you didn't get the joke read about neuroplasticity). Your brain is able to alter its physical and anatomical structure, generate new neurons, repair damaged regions, and rewire different neuronal networks. This means that our learning styles will also change over time. What worked for you a year ago may now be useless. What's more, it might be that you are a multimodal learner so combining different learning styles may have a positive cumulative effect on your studying. Don't be afraid to try mixing techniques, and don't stick to just one! For instance, if you are studying a topic about photosynthesis, read a chapter about it from the textbook, make some flow charts and diagrams in your notes, color different stages of the process with different colors, then watch videos, and ultimately try out a photosynthesis simulation online.

Lastly, it might feel frustrating, let alone time consuming, to jump from one study strategy to another. At the beginning, you might think that drawing charts and copying illustrations from a biology textbook is tedious work. But you know what? You'll soon see how useful that work turned out to be. Just don't give up! Also, don't do what your classmates or friends are doing just because they might be getting better grades or insisting on having a better study strategy than yours. Do only what helps you most.

All in all, find your preferred learning style(s). Unfortunately, none of this blurb applies to you if you aren't willing to put some extra time into actually memorizing what you have been watching, listening or taking notes on. In the next section, I'll give you some insights into different memorization techniques, all of which are related to one or the other learning style.

9 MEMORIZATION TECHNIQUES

> **"What is not started today**
> **is never finished tomorrow."**
> *Johann Wolfgang von Goethe*

It doesn't take a rocket scientist to figure out that your memorization success depends on a few key variables: **Study time** and **Learning quality and efficiency**. You can also put in another very relevant variable, **Procrastination**. Let's do some algebraic fiddling of these variables. And no, you don't need to be a winner of the International Mathematical Olympiad (IMO) to get the following formula:

Study time = Procrastination / Learning quality and efficiency

So what's it all about? You see, the more you procrastinate (i.e. the bigger the numerator), the more time you'll spend studying. But your ultimate goal is to reduce study time as much as you can. How? You can do this easily by maximizing the *learning quality* and *efficiency*. In this chapter, I will tell you how to do the latter.

Have you ever noticed how much memorization biology requires? Compared to physics, math and chemistry, all of which mainly require good logical thinking and problem solving skills, biology is definitely the most theory-dense subject. In fact, I have poured hours upon hours into reading textbooks upon textbooks. We both know that learning doesn't take place by osmosis or diffusion and that the only way to learn is to engage actively in your studying. There are many ways to do this.

You can work on difficult problems that test your understanding and develop your critical thinking. Or you can engage in active reading, which involves highlighting key concepts, taking notes, summarizing the text, and so on. Again, different people prefer different methods, so find something that works for you and stick to it. Over the years, I have identified different techniques that have helped me improve my retention of information and you'll find them below. My favorites include reading about the same concept from several different textbooks and utilizing mnemonics and acronyms. Let's get started, shall we?

1 Create mnemonics

Mnemonics are a very useful learning tool that can help enhance your information retrieval. You know why? When using a mnemonic, you're forming associations between something you already know, and the new information that is otherwise difficult to recall. The mnemonic is meant to activate your memory in order to retrieve the facts that you once saw in your biology textbook. A word of caution: there is no need to endlessly google mnemonics to find the best list for biology. Don't try to memorize random mnemonics that you've found somewhere if it doesn't make any sense to you or if it isn't relatable to your previous experience. This will just double the workload because you'll have to memorize not only the fact itself but also the mnemonic. Let's get one thing straight - each of us is different and we have different previous experiences. Just imagine you're trying to use a mnemonic contrived by your friend. Do you think it will make sense to you? Quite unlikely, because you may not have any associations to make with that mnemonic because you've never experienced what your friend had. Believe me, you can easily make mnemonics yourself.

Before we delve into some techniques for creating mnemonics, let me share one of my personal experiences where mnemonics helped me learn fast. In addition to biology, I'm tremendously in love with languages. I'm a native Lithuanian speaker and I'm somewhat proficient in English (at least I hope I am). I also understand Russian and Spanish, and recently started learning Mandarin Chinese and Korean. Do you want to see how powerful mnemonics are? Let's make a bet. In less than 3 minutes I'll teach you a small part of the Korean alphabet using mnemonics. Deal? To begin with, the Korean alphabet, known as *hangeul*, uses very unique symbols and it consists of 14 consonants and 10 vowels. Ready?

ㄱ sounds like **g** and it looks like a **g**un

ㄴ sounds like **n** and looks like a **n**ose

ㄹ sounds like **l/r** and looks like a **r**attlesnake or **l**inguini

ㅁ sounds like **m** and looks like a **m**ap

ㅎ sounds like **h** and looks like a **h**at

I guess now you're also able to identify at least 5 letters in Korean. Okey, let's learn how to create mnemonics.

First, look at the concept that you want to memorize. Can you tell me what is the first thing that pops into your brain when you see it? Write it down and then frame the mnemonic according to that first thought. The words in a mnemonic may be real or made-up. Use anything that is easy to relate to what you already know. Let me walk you through some examples of acronyms (an acronym is a word that is formulated as an abbreviation from the first letters of different words or phrases) and mnemonics that helped me get the hang of some biology facts. For instance, when I was studying phylogeny, I used this mnemonic:

Keep-Pond-Clear-Or-Fish-Get-Sick

It helped me to remember the taxonomy ranks as the capital letters stand for:

Kingdom-Phylum-Class-Order-Family-Genus-Species.

The next one is a mnemonic that helped me learn the order of the intermediates in the Krebs cycle:

Oh, Citrate Is A Silly Stupid Funny Molecule.

It stands for **O**xaloacetate, **C**itrate, **I**socitrate, **A**lpha-Ketoglutarate, **S**uccinyl CoA, **S**uccinate, **F**umarate, **M**alate. I also used a lot of acronyms to memorize the key amino acids. I remember the basic amino acids by the acronym (and actual word) **HAL**L: **H**istidine-**A**rginine-**L**ysine. **GALVIMP** can help you remember nonpolar non-charged amino acids: **G**lycine, **A**lanine, **L**eucine, **V**aline, **I**soleucine, **M**ethionine, **P**roline. 'Tom Came and Took my **GAS**' encrypts amino acids that are polar but non-charged: **T**hreonine, **C**ysteine, **T**yrosine, **G**lutamine, **A**sparagine, **S**erine. Give it a try and create your own associations to remember information. Rote memorization is both tough and time consuming whereas mnemonics and acronyms make the learning process quick, funny, and pleasurable.

2 Understand what you're learning

Ever noticed how hard it's to remember something that you don't understand? You know where I'm going. To learn a concept, you need to understand it. Inside out. Outside in. I can assure you that things you memorize without fully understanding them won't stay in your head for long. And no, you don't want this. So how do we avoid this?

First, always read the book with a pencil. Underline everything that is confusing and difficult to grasp. Don't ignore these concepts. Then, ask your teacher or your friends about it or consult with the Internet. Find some good discussion forums online or join the Biolympiads Study Group on Google Groups, and discuss any troubles with your olympiad comrades. Remember, first comprehension, then memorization. Never leave anything unclear.

Do you want me to tell you what happened to me once? Understanding all the operons, operators and promoters was really hard for me when I had just started preparing for the olympiad. Specifically, I am talking about all the knockout experiments with lacI-, lacO- etc., mutants, and creating merozygotes to see if the wild type phenotype is restored or not. So out of despair, I just left them. Ignored them. Didn't even try to understand them. And bang! That topic came up in the regional olympiad. Shoot me now. I screwed it up for an obvious reason, but at least I learned a good lesson. Things you don't get will likely come up in the exam (there might even be a Murphy's law about this!). Believe me, it's better to be prepared rather than sorry.

3 Associate names with something you know already

I don't know about you, but this hack is one I rely on all the time and it's truly foolproof. It has a similar effect to mnemonics and acronyms and all of them work by associating things you are learning to something you already know. This powerful technique relies on neuron networks in the brain that already exist, meaning it takes less time to memorize new things.

You might have heard of the study I am about to tell you. In this experiment, subjects were divided into two groups [4]. In the first group, participants were told that the person's last name was "Mr. Farmer," whereas those in the second study group were told that the person was a farmer (his profession). Then, study subjects in both groups were shown the image of a person and they had to remember the word they were told before. Those in the latter group (where participants had to remember a profession) were more likely to recall the name than those in the former (where participants had to remember the surname). You might be wondering why. After all, they all got the same image and same word but their performance still differed.

It turns out that hearing the word 'farmer' as a profession automatically switches on neurons that are associated with this profession and this helps you visualize a person. What comes to your mind when you hear a 'farmer'? To me it links to a guy in his 50s or 60s, unkempt hair, brown moustache, checkered shirts, and a big tummy. Then, by linking what you already know about the farmer, you can develop more mental links to the features of the person in the image. In contrast, the simple name 'Mr. Farmer' pretty much stands alone.

If you really want to break out of the inefficient learn-forget cycle, then apply this associative memory principle whenever you are memorizing something new. Biology is full of incredible, enchanting, and diverse living systems. And that's why it is easy to relate a particular term or concept to common appearances, particular colors or peculiar features. And associations don't have to be biological - they can come from politics, art, or music, among other areas. For instance, a good way to memorize how auxin works is to remember that **auxin** is like **A**nakin Skywalker - both move to the dark side. Take a look at another example. In microbiology, we classify bacteria into Gram-positive and Gram-negative types. The way I remember that Gram-**negative** bacteria are red is because blood is red and when someone is bleeding, the consequences may be **negative**. Gram-**positive** bacteria stain blue. And the sky is blue. When you look at the blue sky, you always feel **positive**, don't you? So when you are memorizing, relate the concepts you are studying to facts that are well-known to you already. These associations will then anchor important biological information in your brain. For a very long time.

Another very beneficial memorization technique is linking together the information that you need to memorize. For example, if you are trying to remember the features of protostomes and deuterostomes, link names and features together. Use your imagination and be creative with

Figure 4 Me Teaching A Fellow Student

words! Funny names are much easier to remember than normal ones, no? For instance, the way I remembered that deuterostomes have enterocoelom and radial and indeterminate cleavage is by this: **INDE**-ut-**ENTE**-**RADI**-ostomes. Still sounds like deuterostomes. A bit. So link the term with characteristics surrounding that word and this will help you remember both.

4 Teach others

When you are trying to memorize a concept, you have to really understand the matter and you must be able to explain it to others using lay words and simple associations. Believe me, teach others and you'll teach yourself. From my own experience, I learnt the most while tutoring others (**Figure 4**).

Here's all you have to do. Gather a group of biology nerds and set up a science club in your school. Design a study plan which clearly outlines what you'll review every time you meet.

Assign topics to all members and each present them to each other. Meet regularly. Support each other during presentations, ask questions, and, most crucially, share your knowledge. Don't go there just to absorb the information like a sponge without giving anything back to your team. Pay it forward!

If setting up a science club sounds like too much work or if you are an introvert (like me) and don't quite like big groups of people, just find a biology study buddy. Draw diagrams and do worksheets together. Teach concepts to each other to help both of you better understand and recall the topics. It's that easy. And the perk of having a study buddy is that he or she will also be a person to whom you are accountable (hey, who wants to disappoint a friend?). This will keep you on railroad tracks to the olympiad.

5 Use all the different senses you've got

When you are trying to remember something, write it down, read it, hear it, draw it, see it, smell it, feel it, experience it, rehearse it, teach it to someone. The list is endless. The more actively you engage with the information you're memorizing, the more likely it's that you'll make crucial connections between the neurons in your brain, allowing you to retain information for longer.

As I mentioned above, I learn best by writing words and sentences by hand many times, i.e. by using a motor and visual component of learning. In fact, scientific evidence shows that writing the same information repeatedly has a significant effect on the encoding specificity of visual-motor information [5]. Other studies also show that hand-writing notes may help retain more information than using electronic devices [6]. Psychology professors from Washington University found that writing notes by hand involves a more comprehensive and deeper processing of the information in the brain than merely typing information into the computer, which requires only shallow information encoding. Additionally, functional magnetic resonance imaging (fMRI) studies have shown that hand-writing stimulates parts of the brain that process and integrate the physical, auditory, and intelligible parts of human learning processes [7]. So yeah, try writing the concept a dozen times and see if you can remember it well.

Apart from writing, a visual component can help, too. Drawing illustrations, graphs, tables, and mind maps can significantly accelerate your memorization process. Psychology professor Karin James from Indiana University studied this in children by giving them the task of replicating a single letter by typing, drawing on plain paper or tracing it over a dotted outline [8]. fMRI studies of these children's brains showed that kids who drew the letters activated three distinct areas of the brain related to learning. In contrast, the brains of those who only traced or typed the letter didn't show the same effect. This experiment suggests that active learning by incorporating drawing has a significant effect on the brain's activity and memorization.

Another good way to learn new information is to buy a small whiteboard and have it in your room. Practice various concepts like the Krebs cycle or gluconeogenesis by drawing and writing down key steps on the whiteboard every so often. This action combines visual and writing modalities, amplifying your learning ability.

6 Use post-it notes or index cards

Write down key concepts and terms and draw figures on post-it notes or index cards. Making the cards is already active learning so this will further reduce the effort needed to memorize facts! Stick your post-it notes where you can see them all the time, for example, on your locker, bedroom walls, doors, or windows (**Figure 5**). Don't forget to read them every time you pass by. You can use colorful post-it notes and categorize them based on the topic. For instance, you can use green sticky notes for plant biology and red for human physiology. This will help you organize information according to different topics.

Figure 5 My Post-it Note Window In My Room

7 Test yourself regularly

Many of us just focus on reading as many biology textbooks as possible, don't we? When you're reading something, at that time it feels like you know everything. And you definitely think you'll remember it forever. But… once you get distracted or review the same material after some time, everything seems completely new. Familiar feeling? I was there, too. To make sure you really remember what you've just read, test yourself regularly by doing worksheets with questions. And to stay accountable, incorporate this activity into your study schedule and give enough time to get the most out of it. On the Biolympiads.com website you'll find thousands of biology olympiad questions that you can use to challenge yourself. Find topic-specific question banks and do them after you read the chapter. All the mistakes you make will help you identify the concepts that you didn't understand and point you in the right direction of what you need to recap.

8 Take regular breaks when memorizing

Take a break every so often (around every 60 to 90 minutes), because your brain can't handle too much information in one go. Go for a walk or do a short workout to activate your muscles and increase circulation to the brain. This will allow your body to recharge. Plus, your eyes will also relax before they must go on to process another hour of intensive reading. Moreover, regular breaks will keep you away from burnout. Even research supports the idea that intermittent breaks can help you regain focus and study more effectively [9].

You might think that breaks are time-consuming and worthless (this is, in fact, what I thought when I was studying for the olympiad). But remember that you cannot stuff your neurons endlessly with new information without giving some time to them to digest it. So, plan your breaks wisely and incorporate them into your study schedule.

9 Experience things you learn practically

The idea of this tip is that you shouldn't just learn from textbooks. Who likes that? It's just too mundane. Besides, memorizing things that you can't relate to demands so much effort. Imagine a situation where you just got your first bike. Would you learn to ride it merely by reading about it in the book for dummies or the user's manual? Most likely not. That's what I truly love about biology - it's such a hands-on field of study that there are many opportunities for you to experience almost everything that you learn from textbooks practically.

Let me give you some suggestions. If you're learning about the cross sections of plants, get access to a microscope and find some slides and a small blade. Pick a dicot and a monocot and make your own slides. Take photos and add them to your notes to remind you of that activity. Or if you're studying molecular biology techniques, like Western blot or chromatography, you can try getting a short internship in a local lab (**Figure 6**). This will help you to memorize the steps and chemicals used in the procedure faster, as you can recall exactly what you did in the experiment. Then, when it comes to the olympiad, you'll have that crucial experience to draw upon when you get any questions related to what you did practically. Plus, remember that in the IBO (and many other biology olympiads), 50% of your final score comes from the practical exam. So, as a bonus, the biology olympiad will help you nail your practical lab skills and become a better scientist.

10 Study when you're at your best

Decide whether you're a morning person or a night owl and find the most productive time for studying. This will ensure you have the maximum concentration to achieve the best results. I prefer studying in the mornings as I am well-rested and full of energy. Interestingly, some studies show, however, that human memory is superior when sleep occurs shortly after learning rather than following a long period of wakefulness [10], the reason being that sleep stabilizes the memories and information that we obtained

Figure 6 One Of My First Dreadful Attempts To Load An Electrophoresis Gel

throughout the day. Surprisingly, it seems that staying awake after you learn something does the opposite - it interferes with memory consolidation. Try studying in the morning and in the evening and see which time of the is best for *you*.

11 Sleep, sleep, sleep

When you are in slow wave sleep, your brain is trying to make sense of what you've learned during the day and consolidates all new information [11]. Put simply, without sleep you cannot put your learned things in your memory. So aim for at least eight hours of sleep every night. Don't sacrifice sleep for the sake of studying. If you don't believe me, do an experiment - stay awake for endless hours and sleep only four to six hours per day. You'll soon see a significant drop in concentration and learning efficiency.

12 Use several textbooks or resources to memorize the same information

This tip is one of my favorites and it helped me build a solid knowledge foundation in biology. Using different textbooks for the same topic exposes you to different words and diagrams that are still about the same subject. This will help you build up a more exact memory as you see different perspectives. To tell you the truth, different books contain slightly different presentations of topics, including different descriptions, meaning that you'll get more information overall if you read two different textbooks rather than just one. Moreover, this tip has an additional benefit - as you are reading a different text, this will definitely keep you interested. Who likes to read the same book a hundred times? Definitely not me. So grab 2-3 books about plants, 2-3 books about human physiology and 2-3 books for genetics to begin with, and review the same chapters from those books to build your knowledge and accelerate memorization.

13 Have a positive attitude

You might be wondering how psychology and your mental state is associated with memorization, but without a positive mindset, you are doomed to fail. Yeah, I can assure you that having a positive attitude will improve your brain capacity to accommodate for new concepts and facts. Study only when you feel you can climb any mountain. Believe in your capabilities and have confidence in yourself and your hard work. Every single minute, hour, day, and week. Always repeat to yourself that *you* can accomplish the targets *you* set.

If, however, on one of the days you don't feel right, don't force yourself to study but instead take a worthwhile day off and do what you usually like to do for relaxation. Go to the swimming pool or meet your friends. Direct your thoughts away from biology for that day. This will give you time to recharge and come back to studying with greater determination and more energy the next day. I ignored those precious days off so don't repeat my mistakes.

14 Find some time to exercise

Numerous studies have shown that regular exercise can reduce stress and anxiety, and significantly enhance your memory [12]. In fact, brain imaging experiments show that some parts of the brain that control thinking and memory are bigger in volume in people who exercise regularly compared to those who don't. I know you're now thinking that you already have almost no time for studying, let alone to exercise. But listen, you can easily incorporate low- to moderate-intensity exercise into your study plan and make this a daily routine. When it's there, you're obligated to take a break and put those muscle sarcomeres on fire.

If you need some more persuasion, here you go: The benefits of exercise arise from the release of growth factors, which are chemicals in the brain that affect the survival and proliferation of neurons [13]. It also enhances the growth of new blood vessels which will increase the whole brain's blood flow. This consequently will improve your cognitive brain health as your hippocampus (the learning and memory center) receives more food and oxygen. So get moving, mate.

15 Turn on the lights

When you're studying, use proper lighting. After all, it's quite depressing to sit in a dark and gloomy room studying, isn't it? Several studies have shown that short exposure to light can improve the brain responses to certain cognitive tasks [14]. In fact, light exposure triggers an activation of the hippocampus where memory consolidation takes place. So switch on a desk lamp, place it opposite the dominant writing hand and feel empowered by the light. If it's summer, go to the garden and study there. Not only will you get some fresh air, but you'll also boost your vitamin D levels which will further accelerate memorization. If you don't believe me, read a meta-analysis published in 2017 by Amraei *et al.* [15]. They showed that vitamin D can protect the nervous system and improve learning. Moreover, they discuss the relationship between hypovitaminosis D and cognitive decline. So you better get your vitamin D levels up to enhance your learning!

16 Repeat, repeat, repeat

You've probably heard of the saying that repetition is the mother (or father) of learning. So keep reviewing and repeating things you learned some time ago because the information will be soon forgotten. Studies support the observation that the more you encounter something, the more likely you are to recall it [16]. This hack relies on working memory. Your neurons must distinguish between important and unimportant information. Unimportant information will be erased and forgotten and important information will be consolidated and retained. One of the ways your brain decides what to keep and store as long-term memory is by analyzing information that it has processed multiple times. This obviously means that the more years you spend on the biology olympiad preparation, the more chances you'll have to actually review the same information. In fact, when I read a general biology textbook for the first time, I was so frustrated and I thought I would never learn all that information. It was just too much. But as the years went by, I revisited the information again and again and it just became second nature.

17 Study by 'chunking'

Memorizing is like eating. We tend to remember things better if we learn information in small chunks rather than trying to cram all the concepts from the chapter in at once. Think about how you eat, for example, your lunch. You chew the food in small bites and then spend some time swallowing before you take another bite. Similarly, when you're trying to take in a lot of information at once, your working memory physically can't hold all the details you just crammed. Those extra facts outside of your working memory capacity are just lost. So don't be a greedy gnome and 'eat' your book slowly, chewing properly, and swallowing the information carefully.

18 Space out your learning

Studies have shown that spacing out your learning activities results in better information retention than massing them together [17]. Don't let your own brain trick you - you might feel that when you stuff your brain with as many facts as possible in a very short period of time, you'll remember them for the rest of your life. But that's not the case. Why not? Immediate short-term retrieval fluency after you just memorized a lot of things in one go doesn't have long-term effects so it won't help you retain information. Instead, try to revise the same chapter or topic several times for short periods which are spread evenly across multiple days or months. Don't spend a long time revising the same material once and then never review it again as this might not be helpful. An hour here and an hour there will make your learning journey more efficient.

19 Read out loud

Now this one has never worked for me. But guess how I learned about this memorization method? Let me tell you the whole story. One day I was in my room and heard a quiet whispering voice similar to the one that you can hear in the church when someone is praying. "What the heck?", I thought. Apparently, it was my sister in the room next door. It really worried me since we don't practice religion at all. I rushed into her room all covered in sweat and hyperventilating and, while trying to catch my breath, asked her what was going on. False alarm. Phew! It turned out that she was revising for her chemistry exam. And reading through her notes out loud was what helped her best to memorize.

Essentially, in this technique you read out loud to yourself most of the time to understand and remember what you've just read. Let me back this up with some robust scientific evidence because we biologists love evidence, don't we? In 2017, scientists published an interesting study in the journal *Memory* [18]. In a nutshell, they set up four experiments:

1) participants heard themselves reading aloud words that were recorded earlier
2) participants were reading aloud
3) subjects were hearing someone else speak
4) subjects were reading silently

Scientists found that those who spoke aloud had better recall than those who listened to their own recordings. That means that just listening to the information isn't enough to improve memory but both speaking and hearing helps encode the memory more strongly. When you add a production element (motor in the form of speech and auditory in the form of hearing) to a word or a phrase that you are trying to memorize, this word or sentence becomes more memorable in your brain. Not surprisingly, those who listened to others or read in silence didn't show better recall.

The list of tips for improving memorization is not exhaustive and I am sure you might have your own tricks, too. Use anything that helps *you*! And keep in mind that memory is like a muscle - the more you train it, the better it gets! So during the first weeks of studying it might be very hard to memorize things, but, as you advance, remembering the information becomes much easier. In fact, to me, Campbell once seemed to be a frightfully tedious textbook with a dreadful number of pages that I would never be able to memorize. But you know they say first times always cut the deepest. So keep pushing and it'll get easier. Trust me, perseverance is essential if you really want to succeed not only in the biology olympiad, but also in your academic and personal life.

The next chapter is fairly related to what you learned in this chapter. Raise your hand if you've ever found yourself studying until very late for a test. Cramming can be a lifesaver if you only have a few weeks left before the biology olympiad and you need to memorize a ton of facts in a limited amount of time. Note that the tips in the next chapter are there just like a life vest that can help you temporarily, but if you want to swim across the ocean, you need to learn how to swim without any aids. This means that the best way to learn the material is to consistently repeat and practice it for a long time. Believe or not, cramming isn't a sustainable way of studying so try to avoid it if you can.

10 CRAMMING

> **"Live as if you were to die tomorrow.**
> **Learn as if you were to live forever."**
> *Mahatma Gandhi*

In an ideal situation, you'd have a lot of free time to prepare for a biology olympiad. But… with extracurricular activities like sports, music classes, and family time, you might only have a few hours per week for studying for the olympiad. Then, imagine that the test is just a few weeks from today and you haven't even started reviewing the study material. Relax mate! If you ever find yourself in such a situation (and we've all been there), there are some useful tips and tricks that will help you get the most out of your limited time.

It's important to realize, however, that cramming for a biology olympiad may work on a short-term basis only. The truth is you *shouldn't* use this method as your main learning style. Trust me, it's not at all effective in the long run and can do more harm than good. Reason being, after endless hours of studying and sleepless nights you'll drain your body like hypertonic soil drains the roots of the plant. Plus, cramming before the olympiad almost guarantees that you'll forget everything a week after. How's that? Reviewed material will leave your brain as quickly as it's stuffed in there (this is similar to Starling's law in cardiovascular physiology which states that the more blood fills the ventricles, the more blood will leave the heart during systole). However, sometimes cramming is unavoidable, so focus on maximizing the benefits of cramming when you have no other option. So how do we do this?

1 Have a plan (as always!)

If you decide to cram for several weeks, you first need to be really efficient with your time and fit in as many hours of studying as possible. For those couple of weeks, sacrifice partying and hanging out with friends. Spend as much time in as possible to avoid any distractions. Your best friends and family will support you and encourage you, so don't worry about them at this point. Next, allocate equal time to all biology topics.

2 Use handouts, not textbooks

Do you think you'll have time to read the whole textbook(s) in one or two weeks? Dream on… When you're cramming before the exam, focus on reading your notes and not textbooks. I particularly love presentations as they give you concise visual information in small, digestible amounts. Google something like 'cellular respiration ppt' and you will get many results. Use only reliable sources, usually those published on university websites or on reputable scientific websites. There are also many readymade textbook-specific notes out there that cover the general concepts so all you need to do is just find them and use them.

3 Focus on diagrams and illustrations

After you review the notes for all the key biology topics (cell biology, biochemistry, animal anatomy and physiology, plant biology, evolution, ecology, and ethology), skim through diagrams and charts from the key textbooks. Diagrams are really good if you're trying to grasp really complex concepts quickly. Don't ignore them - instead, analyze them carefully. Especially review cross sections of plant organs, animal anatomy and histology as well as phylogenetic trees. As the biology olympiad now puts a lot of emphasis on biochemistry, molecular and cell biology, review the chemical structures of the most prevalent biomolecules including carbohydrates, amino acids, nucleic acids, different types of lipids. Don't forget commonly encountered coenzymes and cofactors like coenzyme A, NADH, and $FADH_2$ and other physiologically important molecules mentioned in the textbooks, including hemoglobin, cytochromes and chlorophyll, to name a few.

4 Use different styles of learning

When you want to memorize as many things as possible in a very short period of time, I recommend utilizing different types of learning (see section 'Learning Styles'). So by using your notes, you are using your reading and visual skills. By analyzing and drawing your own diagrams and charts, you are using your kinesthetic skills (for this you can buy a small portable whiteboard where you can draw different things every day). Then, utilize your listening skills by watching some online biology videos and/or university lectures. For example, MIT OpenCourseWare has some amazing free study resources appropriate for the level of the biology olympiad.

My most favorite courses that are relevant to the biology olympiad include:

5.07SC Biological Chemistry I (Fall 2013)

7.01SC Fundamentals of Biology (Fall 2011)

7.012 Introduction to Biology (Fall 2004)

7.013 Introductory Biology (Spring 2006)

7.013 Introductory Biology (Spring 2013)

7.014 Introductory Biology (Spring 2005)

7.016 Introductory Biology (Fall 2014)

7.03 Genetics (Fall 2004)

7.06 Cell Biology (Spring 2007)

5 Make a checklist

To keep yourself on track during your cramming marathon, make a checklist for each topic that you need to review. Tick each checkbox after you revise that topic. This will do two things. First, it'll boost your motivation because you'll clearly see your progress. Secondly, it'll indicate where you stand in your limited cramming session and how much still needs to be done, stopping you from procrastinating.

6 Sleep more

The key tip for cramming is a good night's sleep. Research shows that learning requires consolidation that occurs when we are asleep [19]. Lack of sleep can cause reading fatigue and confusion of concepts. When you are exhausted, you won't be able to connect new information to what you've learned earlier. So do get a really good night's sleep every day when you're cramming and don't replace your sleeping hours with endless hours of studying, deal? Believe me, it's much better to go into a biology olympiad test under-prepared (at least you can use your logic) than sleep-deprived (which means that your brain can't function properly and logic won't work). Leave 24 hours biology-free before the test and do something else you enjoy to recharge for the next day. This will also help avoid burnout and confusion in your brain. You'll be surprised by the results!

7 Have short breaks

Keep in mind that studying too much can sometimes be as serious a mistake as not studying enough when you're cramming. Don't overwork and plan to allocate time for rest and other activities in your cramming schedule. So if you commit to do very intensive cramming for some time, take a look at **Table 1** for a suggested revision timetable.

To end with, in general most of the concepts you absorb during your cram session will be stored in your brain as short term memory and probably won't be converted to long term memory. This means that once you have walked out of the olympiad test, you'll forget everything you crammed. I'm exaggerating a bit, but my point is that cramming may be enough to get you through the first round of the olympiad but, as you walk away from the test room, ask yourself what you've actually learnt by cramming. If the answer isn't satisfying, prepare to get serious for the next round. Before you start, learn how to organize your study material in the next chapter to maximize your studying efficiency.

Table 1 One Week Long Intensive Biology Study Schedule

WEEK DAY	MORNING	AFTERNOON	EVENING
MONDAY	School	1 pm - 2 pm (lunch break)	5 pm - 10 pm
TUESDAY	School	1 pm - 2 pm (lunch break)	5 pm - 10 pm
WEDNESDAY	School	1 pm - 2 pm (lunch break)	5 pm - 10 pm
THURSDAY	School	1 pm - 2 pm (lunch break)	5 pm - 10 pm
FRIDAY	School	1 pm - 2 pm (lunch break)	5 pm - 10 pm
SATURDAY	9 am - 1 pm	2 pm - 5 pm	7 pm - 10 pm
SUNDAY	9 am - 1 pm	2 pm - 5 pm	7 pm - 10 pm

11 ORGANIZING YOUR STUDY MATERIAL

"Entropy is constantly increasing."
2nd Law of Thermodynamics

Textbooks aren't the only source of information you need for the olympiad preparation. The Internet is filled with various presentations, lecture notes, worksheets, etc. for any topic of biology. And if you're not one who can learn solely from textbooks, these additional study resources will help you get a solid grasp of different subjects. Now, imagine a situation where you download all these awesome resources and save them in different places in your computer. Nothing sucks more than trying to find a presentation or handout in the laptop with Ctrl+F a week before the olympiad, only to realize that you either didn't save it or saved it somewhere without a proper name. Smack!

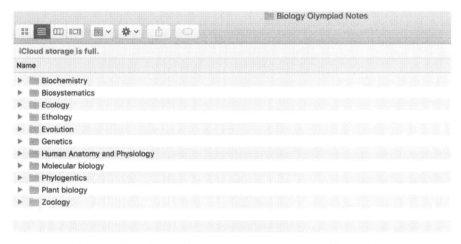

Figure 7 Subfolder Structure For Biology Olympiad Notes

To avoid going through this hell (although Churchill once said, "... *keep going*"), meticulously organize your study files. My biology olympiad folder occupies around 93.96 GB. If yours is of a similar size, keeping your documents organized will make your life easier. You can do all of this on your desktop or, ideally, in the cloud. What I like about the online storage cloud is that your files will be accessible from any device. Just imagine yourself getting stranded on an island in the middle of nowhere with your smartphone and even WiFi! As you're alone and there is (obviously) nothing else to do, you can lay on the sand, access any of your biology folders, and start studying. In addition, some online platforms will allow you to live-edit documents which is really useful if you need to add some new things to your notes without having to create millions of new files. So find the digital platform that you like the most and start using it. This will help you easily dig out your documents when you need them.

So how do you set up your biology olympiad file storage system? Create a folder called *'Biology Olympiad'* (**Figure 7**) and then add subfolders for all the major biology topics like *'Human Physiology and Anatomy'*, *'Plant Biology'*, *'Ecology'*, etc. Next, divide each subfolder into sub-subfolders: *'Handouts'*, *'Presentations'*, and *'Worksheets'* (**Figure 8**). Whenever you download a file, add it to the correct subfolder or sub-subfolder. Don't ignore this crucial step! This hierarchy of folders will accelerate your topic-wise studying as you'll have worksheets and presentations for that particular topic ready for you to review whenever you need it.

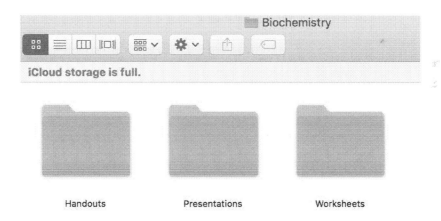

Figure 8 Sub-subfolder Structure For Biology Olympiad Notes

Once your folders are all set up, you've got to train yourself to save all files you download in the right place. It goes without saying that you need to learn to name them correctly so that you can search for them later without fuss. Keep your files in order and don't get in the habit of increasing entropy in your folders as this will ruin all your hard work. Yeah, it sounds like quite a bit of work but in the end you will thank yourself for having neatly organized biology olympiad notes.

Lastly, I would recommend creating a spreadsheet with various links to different biology websites for review. Sometimes, you can't download the files from the Internet and if you want to review that material again, save the link in your spreadsheet. Again, be organized and set it up in a neat fashion (for instance, as shown in **Figure 9**). It can be very useful to have a column for comments next to the link to insert a description of what exactly you want to review from that page.

Molecular Biology		Plant Biology		Biochemistry		Human Anatomy & Physiology	
Link	Comments	Link	Comments	Link	Comments	Link	Comments
http://people.eku.edu/ritchisong/301notes1.htm	An overview that has links and explanation of every topic listed in the International Biology Olympiad manual.	http://www2.estrellamountain.edu/faculty/farabee/biobk/BioBookDiversity_5.html	Indepth study guide with review questions and links on the plants.	http://www.emc.maricopa.edu/faculty/farabee/biobk/BiobookGlyc.html	Fermentation pathways	http://recap.ltd.uk/podcasting/sciences/biology2110.php	Introductory undergraduate lectures in anatomy and physiology – Podcast Lectures
http://learn.genetics.utah.edu/	Genetics overview	http://www.ableweb.org/volumes/vol-19/9-yeung.pdf	PDF of description and examples of botanical microtechniques.	http://instruct1.cit.cornell.edu/courses/biomi290/ASM/glycolysis.der	Glycolysis animation	http://bcs.whfreeman.com/thelifewire/content/chp50/5002002.html	Insulin and glucose regulation
http://www.johnkyrk.com/DNAtranslation.html	Animation of RNA translation.	http://www.herbarium.lsu.edu/keys/visual-keys.html	Interactive identfication key for plants with global collections. By keying, the user can learn a great deal about plants, such as stomate number, location found, and much more.	https://www.chem.purdue.edu/courses/chm333/	Biochemistry problem sets	http://www.gastro.net.au/frame_dugestive.html	General Gastrointestinal tract overview
http://www.johnkyrk.com/mitosis.html	Mitosis	https://water.usgs.gov/edu/watercycletranspiration.html	Description of water cycle and transpiration. Interactive Water Cycle map at the bottom of the page provides information ground, water, evaporation, and other factors.	http://home.apu.edu/~simons/Bio101/biochem.htm	General biochemistry overview	http://www.besthealth.com/besthealth/bodyguide/reftext/html/immu_sys_fin.html	Solid immune system overview that matches what is in Campbell.

Figure 9 Spreadsheet With Links To Different Biology Study Resources

Once you have all your folders sorted, it's time to learn how to make your own notes to accelerate learning and improve your revision efficiency.

12 NOTE TAKING TIPS

> *"Knowing is not enough; we must apply.*
> *Willing is not enough; we must do."*
> *Johann Wolfgang von Goethe*

Many people ask me whether it's useful to take notes and if yes, how to do it successfully. The good news is there are so many websites on the Internet from which you can just download, copy-paste, or buy well-digested notes ready for your neurons to endocytose. But here's the interesting thing: do you remember our discussion about different learning types (hint: kinesthetic method)? Awesome! So you see, research shows that note taking actually improves learning [20]. According to the encoding hypothesis, when you take notes, the processing that takes place in your brain will improve information retention. And the best part? Good note taking skills might help you consolidate the information and also stay organized and focused on reading, which will reduce your study time. What's more, notes are good for last-minute revision when you are desperate to review topics you aren't totally comfortable with. So what do you need to do to make your notes actually useful to your learning process?

1 Write clearly and legibly to reduce entropy in your notes

Don't you just hate it when your notes are full of words you can't even read? Let me guess, you use the second law of thermodynamics as an excuse, don't you? Yes, constantly increasing entropy in the universe is a real thing, but, for the sake of success in the olympiad, write neat and legible notes. Sound like a waste of time? Let me ask how long you spend trying to read the illegible bits. I bet cracking the illegible text probably takes more than making legible notes. So once you've nailed good note taking, you'll save a ton of time during revision. However, not all people have perfect handwriting, including me. If you have unreadable handwriting, write everything in capitals.

2 Avoid typing

I know you, like many other students, might love to type your notes on the computer. It's faster, tidier, and produces fewer mistakes. But do you remember I shared some published studies about typing your notes and learning in the sections above? An accumulating body of research shows that writing your notes by hand helps you learn faster. As a matter of fact, this process triggers different cognitive processes in the brain that are related to learning. So don't be tempted to use your laptop to make notes. If you're still not convinced, here is another study. Researchers from Princeton University and the University of California split a class of students into two groups: One was instructed to take notes with a computer and the other was assigned to write the notes out by hand [21]. Not surprisingly, students who used computers worked faster and made longer notes. However, when scientists challenged the students' memory for factual details and conceptual understanding of the learned material, it turned out that those who had written their notes by hand excelled in all of these tasks. So, use the old-fashioned method with a pen and paper when taking your notes.

3 Use loose leaf paper and note down just one topic per sheet

Notebooks are good but they restrict your freedom to change the order of your notes or add more information later on. Instead, use loose papers that you can shuffle around in your folder. Also, note down only one topic per sheet and don't mix different topics on the same page. For example, if you're studying the heart, outline all key concepts about the heart on the same page and take another paper to make notes on something like the endocrine or immune system. This will help you organize your notes into topics and will enable you to create a good table of contents. Being able to find what you need quickly is one of the ingredients of efficient studying.

4 Don't copy and paste the book

Be selective in your choice of what to note down. Try using short text fragments and abbreviations. Don't just rewrite the entire book, got it? Making your notes too long is as bad as making them too short, so try to find the happy medium. I know it's very easy to turn into a mindless copying zombie when you're taking notes, but try to avoid this just like anions avoid other negatively charged things. How? Allocate just *one* A4 page per topic and don't allow yourself to breach this rule.

5 Use bullet points and avoid writing paragraphs of text

Not only are bullet points easier to spot and review, but they're also more concise, meaning you'll spend less time on revision later. Use different indentations to visually organize information. Always strive to avoid clutter on your paper. What if you took your notes in such a way where you:

- Put main ideas at the top level

    ◦ And nested supporting facts and figures below.

    ◦ In the end, your notes will have a clear hierarchical outline of particular topics.

    ◦ This is pretty easy to read and review, isn't it?

- Told you!

6 Use highlighters or colorful pens to sort information

It doesn't matter whether you have any artistic blood in your circulatory system, but just highlight, highlight, highlight. You can also color code different topics so that each color has a specific meaning or reference to a particular topic. Let me give you some examples. You can use red color for notes about the cardiovascular system as it's usually linked to blood. And take a green pen for plant biology notes. This will help you recall biological information better. Yippee! Don't believe me? Research shows that colors play a significant role in enhancing learning performance [22]. Furthermore, using color results in improved memory abilities. Say goodbye to those boring black-and-white notes and hello to colors.

7 Don't leave mistakes

This is related to the first tip. Untidy notes can be a huge hindrance to effective studying. You can easily lose the flow of ideas when you see black spots or scribbles all over your notes. So don't go there. If you make mistakes, get another piece of paper and just rewrite that page. Although it's time consuming, you'll be grateful to yourself later. Plus, by writing the same information again, you'll process those facts a second time and this will serve as revision on its own.

8 Develop a system of abbreviations and symbols

Develop your own set of symbols and abbreviations that make sense to you. For instance, instead of 'female', use '♀', instead of 'increase' use '↑', and instead of the 'electron transport chain', just use the abbreviation 'ETC'. Some other common signs include '=' to indicate similarity and '&' for 'and'. These small abbreviations capture your attention and keep you focused. And even better, they will keep your notes concise. Isn't it much easier to read just one page instead of two?

9 Draw, draw, draw in your notes

Instead of just writing dreadfully long paragraphs of text, convert the text into diagrams. For example, draw the Krebs or Calvin cycle, nephron tubules, the classification of white blood cells or any other concepts you are reading about. This visual information will help you immensely in seeing the bigger picture of key biological processes. Somehow, remembering a diagram is often easier than memorizing text, isn't it? The drawing process itself will act as a method of relaxation, allowing you to recuperate and recharge for the next hour of reading.

You can also create mind maps. To begin with, put an "umbrella" definition or term in the center of the page and keep branching out from it by drawing lines. Then, add information to flesh out that core biological concept. Alternatively, you can use the flowchart method where you put the main concept at the top of the page and nest relevant information and details directly under it in bullet points.

10 Underline key phrases and circle key words in your notes

If you want to identify the most critical parts of the text and stay concentrated on crucial facts, then underline the text you're summarizing. Use colorful pens or pencils. It'll stand out better and help you remember key information quicker as colors have high affinity for your attention (now you know why aposematic coloration in animals works!).

11 Leave spaces and lines between the key concepts

Learning is a dynamic process and you'll often have some additional stuff to add to your notes. You'll probably read a ton of different textbooks and watch many scientific videos during your preparation. This means that you'll always be exposed to the new material. And if you want to remember all those new things, you'll probably want to write them down. So leave some space after each paragraph and in the margins for new information to be added later. This will do two things:

1. It'll keep your notes tidy as you won't need to scribble additional facts in miniature and usually illegible letters.

2. It'll help you read the notes quicker as you won't need to try to decode your teeny-tiny handwriting.

12 Use catchy titles to draw your attention to key concepts

Give suitable headings to the paragraphs and titles to the notes. This will set your brain on that particular topic and keep you focused on exactly what you're about to read. Won't it also help you quickly find specific topics and concepts? You can use different colors for titles to make them easy to notice.

13 Use post-its for adding additional details to your notes

Imagine you found another interesting book about biochemistry but already have a solid set of notes. Even worse, you find something new and you'd like to note it down but you didn't leave any free space on the paper. Breathe! Just jot down the new facts on a post-it note and stick it to the appropriate page. Woohoo! This will keep you miles away from clutter.

14 Write in English (or any other language)

I bet many of you who are reading this book aren't native English speakers. Same here. And you know very well how important foreign languages are, don't you? What I highly advise you to do when taking notes is to use English textbooks. Learn the language at the same time as you learn biology! Believe me, you'll kill two birds with one stone. Firstly, and the most important, you will gather enough scientific knowledge to stand out from the crowd when you apply to a university. Secondly, you'll be able to use your scientific English in any interview or daily communication if you ever go abroad. And don't limit yourself to English. Perhaps you want to learn another language like German or Russian? There are tons of biology textbooks in these languages, so use them to study and make notes from.

To end this section, my answer to the question whether it's useful to takes notes is yes! And I can assure you that there is no right or wrong way to make good notes. For some inspiration, take a look at one page of my notes in **Figure 10**, where I summarized key processes of cellular respiration. Keep your notes brief, well-organized, and tidy. And most importantly, don't forget to review them regularly.

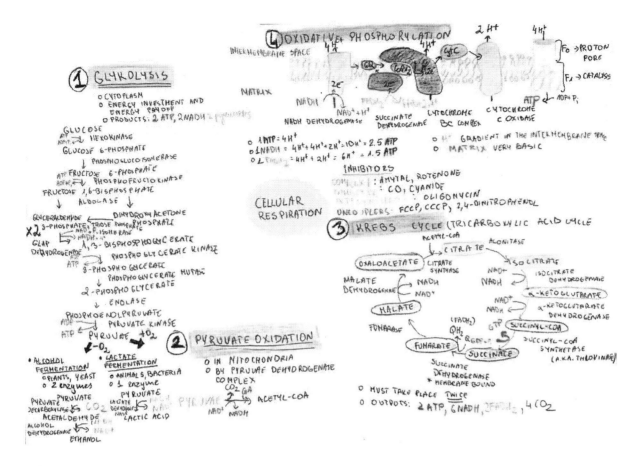

Figure 10 My Notes On Cellular Respiration

13 CRITICAL THINKING SKILLS

> **"The mind is not a vessel to be filled,**
> **but a fire to be kindled."**
> *Plutarch*

You might have been thinking that the biology olympiad is all about rote memorization. I guess that might be due to the breadth of topics. Or maybe your teacher or old past papers gave you that misleading impression. No! No! No! The biology olympiad isn't only about parrot learning (no offense to parrots). So what's it all about? In short, it was designed to challenge your ability to apply your knowledge to different, usually unfamiliar situations and scenarios, understand data, interpret results of scientific experiments, and draw reasonable conclusions from information given. In fact, the majority of exam questions in the IBO mainly focuses on reasoning, problem solving, and understanding [23]. Because of this very reason, you aren't expected to know everything in advance and the IBO exams encourage the participants to learn during the competition. Honestly, you're given a once-in-a-lifetime (sometimes two-in-a-lifetime as you can take part in the IBO only twice) opportunity to learn on the spot. Want to know how to develop those critical thinking skills?

Well, critical thinking, just like (almost) all other things in life, can be learned - but it requires meticulous practice. Do you think you could become a ballet dancer just by reading a book about how to dance? My point? You need to roll up your sleeves and do critical thinking and problem solving yourself, rather than merely trying to find a book about critical thinking with a list of strategies that you can cram. The more tests and questions you do, the better critical thinking skills you'll develop.

In the olympiad, you'll be tested on your understanding and ability to apply biological concepts. Thus, practice and learn to draw and analyze graphs, diagrams, figures, and tables.

Learn to interpret the data given and synthesize well-grounded conclusions. What's more, instead of just accepting information at face value, in the exam you'll need to be able to critically analyze the information by questioning every single word (raise questions such as *Why? How? Are there any alternative explanations?*). So how do you critically analyze the question and options? Follow the steps below to help you critically evaluate a question in the olympiad.

1 Read the question actively

Gather all the information from the question and be open-minded. Highlight, circle, and underline the parts of the question that are important. The worst thing you can do while solving problems is to passively read the question and expect to capture key details. So arm yourself with a highlighter or a pencil!

2 Understand all terms and words

This is why you need to have a solid foundation of biology knowledge. If you don't understand both general and more topic-specific terms and phrases, you'll find it difficult to select the correct answer. In fact, erroneous conclusions when solving problems usually stem from inadequate factual biology knowledge. So keep reviewing biology textbooks and building that knowledge of all topics. A good example is question #12 in the IBO 2012 Theoretical Test Paper 2, which tests your knowledge of the acid growth hypothesis in plants.

3 Analyze and question the methods by which data was collected

Question the source of facts, check if selective inclusion or exclusion of data was performed, and scrutinize the methods by which facts were derived. Look at the question and check if the facts come from a well-controlled experiment or merely from random observations. Also check if the experiments were performed correctly and whether the experimental method could lead to biased results. In biology, different environmental conditions (e.g., temperature, salinity, sunlight), habitat, or species specimen can (and often does) alter experimental results.

4 Analyze the graphs and tables

In fact, tables and graphs can give you a lot of information so notice different trends (increases/decreases/no changes of numbers). For example, a bell-shaped curve will typically indicate that you have a random sample and normal distribution. A sigmoidal curve is linked to the carrying capacity of an environment (a logistic curve) or oxygen dissociation curve. A hyperbolic curve indicates saturation of enzymes or when some kind of limiting factor in the environment is needed to overcome the plateau. A concave upward curve is seen with exponentially increasing functions, as occurs during the log phase of bacterial growth. Sine-wave-like curves are typically linked to circadian rhythms or a negative feedback mechanism. Hypothesize why such patterns occurred and what they could mean in the context of the question. Finally, don't use your gut feeling when analyzing graphs and tables with real data. Derive your conclusions *only* from the information given. For a good example where to apply this tip, check out question #12 from the IBO 2014 Theoretical Test Part A.

5 Connect given facts by drawing models, diagrams, and pathways

The point is that you need to understand what the data is actually showing. In the olympiad, the questions tend to be quite convoluted (especially when it comes to biochemistry and molecular biology), so spend a few minutes on jotting down a model or pathway from the information given. This will allow you to piece together a scientific puzzle. Try to apply this tip to question #3 from the IBO 2008 Theoretical Test Part B about apoptosis.

6 Evaluate conclusions

Analyze your conclusions and ask yourself if the data supports them. Find supporting information for every single statement. Think about alternative conclusions that could be made from the same facts.

7 Beware of hidden assumptions and biases

Don't let some common beliefs or biases cloud your judgment. Critically evaluate the simplistic or most obvious option as these are traps for those who like to guess. Want an example? Well, a common misconception in biology is that if two species resemble each other morphologically, they are most likely evolutionarily related. However, that's not the case as species derived from different ancestors may be similar due to convergent evolution. The key concept that you need to be able to apply in such questions is the biological species concept which states that if we have two organisms, we could classify them as the same species only if they produce viable and fertile offspring despite any morphological similarities.

8 Think about multiple causes and effects

Yep, the simple or most obvious answer is usually not the correct one. Ditch simplistic thinking when you are taking the olympiad paper and consider all of the possible factors and their relative contributions to the conclusion in question. Be careful about utilizing dualistic thinking, which has only two possible viewpoints like black and white or good and bad. Biology is a broad and very diverse field so always look for a third or fourth explanation or possibility.

9 Beware of thought stoppers

Look out for words or sentences that look persuasive and are very attractive (e.g., 'this experiment proves x, y, z' or 'the flies must have x, y, z'). Such phrases actually stop you from thinking critically and instead trigger an emotional acceptance of an argument, not a logical one. Again, in such situations a highlighter will help you spot those keywords easier.

10 Correlation doesn't necessarily mean causation

You can be easily hooked by some obvious correlations but remember how in biology the same effect can be triggered by several different factors. Let me give you an example of a study of hormone replacement therapy (HRT) with women participants. HRT was once praised for its effects on decreasing the risk of coronary heart diseases (CHD) [24]. However, further randomized studies identified no relationship between cardiovascular diseases and HRT [25]. So why did people think otherwise before? It turned out that HRT was usually prescribed to women with higher socioeconomic statuses who had better quality of diet and exercise, which contributed to their lower risk of CHD.

11 Make an educated guess

Using the information in the question, you can often rule out some of the statements and narrow down your options (for tips on how to do this, see the section titled 'Test Taking Techniques'). Beware of statements in the options that are:

- Contrary to the main concept or to the data in the graphs and tables
- Beyond the question, i.e. their validity depends on additional information that isn't given in the question
- Simpleton - such a statement may appear too obvious or too simple
- Illogical - such a statement will be vague or defy common biological truths and concepts

Strive to critically analyze every statement using your knowledge of biology and the information presented in the question. Then, rule out the incorrect ones and make a guess from the remaining options.

To put all of these tips into practice, take past olympiad papers and analyze each question step by step. The next section, 'Problem Solving Skills', ties in nicely with this section about critical thinking. In fact, these two skills are inseparable in the biology olympiad and, not surprisingly, both can be developed at the same time by doing practice problems.

14 PROBLEM SOLVING SKILLS

"Each problem that I solved became a rule, which served afterwards to solve other problems."
Rene Descartes

Haven't you noticed that, most of the time, answering multiple-choice questions in the biology olympiad is about application (I'm talking about the latest papers, not the ones published like a decade ago)? Anyone can cram the entire textbook but not everyone can use higher cognitive skills to answer the questions that don't require just pure recall. If you've had a chance to look at the latest biology olympiad papers, you've probably noticed that in fact questions are designed to differentiate students according to their cognitive abilities. Now, you're probably scratching your head and wondering how they do this. Let me give you such an example:

Imagine we have three trees of the same species. All were cut at the same height. Based on the tree stem cross sections shown below, indicate which statements are correct and which ones are incorrect.

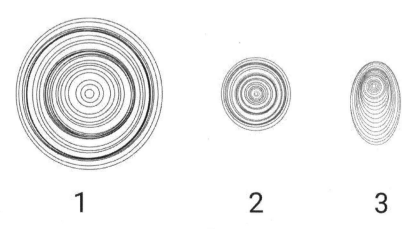

A. Trees 1 and 2 may be found growing in the same area whereas Tree 3 may grow in a different area.

B. Trees 2 and 3 had a rough time during the first fifteen years and grew very slowly.

C. Tree 3 likely experienced more climate variation than Tree 1.

D. Tree 3 is likely older than tree 2 because its cross section is bigger.

Select your answers before you look at the explanations below.

You see, when those smart kids get a hard question, they look for deep, conceptual features, and relate them to what they already know. In the meantime, others tend to base their answer on some superficial features that are irrelevant. So you know that annual tree rings allow us to evaluate tree's age and the conditions under which the plant grew. Statement A is TRUE because you can see that Trees 1 and 2 have the same pattern of growth rings (they both have two darker rings which may indicate bad growth conditions), whereas Tree 3 has a different pattern of rings with no dark parts (meaning it didn't suffer those two periods of bad years). Statement B is also TRUE because you can see that Trees 2 and 3 indeed are smaller than Tree 1. This might mean that they had less water or nutrients or maybe they grew in a shaded area so could not add as much biomass.

Statement C is the one where you need to apply your problem solving skills. You can see that Tree 3 definitely looks different and it has the off-center pith while Tree 1 has regular circularly arranged annual rings. Just by looking at the superficial appearance, you would probably say TRUE, no? A real problem solver would look deeper. Notice, Tree 1 has two areas with very dense annual rings. A problem solver would then ask *why*. Maybe the plant did not have enough sun? Or nutrients? Or maybe it was too dry outside? Now, look at the ring pattern of Tree 3. What do you see? All the rings are in a much more regular pattern in terms of thickness, indicating that Tree 3 didn't experience periods of bad years as did Tree 1 and Tree 2. The reason why Tree 3 looks weird may be because some kind of heavy external object was leaning against the tree and thus the tree grew more to the opposite side to counteract that physical stress. Or it might be that the wind was only blowing from one direction and thus the wood grew faster on the side away from the wind than on the side facing the wind. We can therefore conclude that statement C is actually FALSE.

Intuitively, statement D appears to be logical. Cross section of Tree 3 is slightly bigger. If the tree grows for a longer period of time, its diameter would be larger than that of the younger plant, no? Before making a final decision, a real problem solver would always ask *'why?'*, *'how?'*, *'what if?'*, *'does that apply all the time?'*. What if Tree 2 and Tree 3 are of the same age but Tree 2 doesn't have enough nutrients or light to keep up with the growth of Tree 3? How can you test this? Count the annual rings and you'll see that they're of the same age. This might mean that

Tree 3 is growing under conditions where there is plenty of light, minerals, and water, whereas Tree 2 is growing in a more deprived area. So statement D is FALSE.

Problem Solving Strategy

Now that you've seen an example of problem solving in the biology olympiad, let's get back to the crux of the topic - how to develop problem solving skills. Well... Problem solving itself is comprised of two components:

- knowledge of problem solving strategies, and

- conceptual knowledge (in our case about biology)

The latter can be improved by reading textbooks and building a solid understanding of key biological concepts (check sections 'Memorization Techniques' and 'Reading a Biology Textbook'). Let me emphasize this - it's not how much you memorize, it's how much you internalize. I know I screwed up my lame attempt at rhyming, but the point is that it's always about how much you remember and retain, not how long or how many books you read.

The second component of problem solving is knowledge of problem solving strategies. You won't believe me, but you're the one who knows all the strategies. I don't. You do. Let me explain what I mean by this. Imagine you want (and you're committed, right?) to learn how to solve biology problems. Just like with critical thinking, by far the best thing you can do is to solve actual problems (for instance, past papers or practice problems from textbooks). See, just like a kid won't become a football player by reading books, you won't become a good problem solver by reading some instructions on the Internet (let alone from this book).

Now, let me tell you a gigantic secret. These hours spent on solving past papers and worksheets will help *you* amass various tricks and techniques for biology olympiads that work for *you*. Not to mention the fact that it'll hone your problem solving intuition. It's *that* personal! What works for me probably won't work for you. So you got this now - you do the past papers and find the strategies that help *you* come up with the correct answers. You might now be wondering how on earth you'll come up with all those stupid strategies. Imagine that you were always an awful problem solver and now I'm telling you that they are stashed in your brain. How do you get them out into the daylight? Simple, but I bet you've never done this before! Listen mate, here's the secret:

Train yourself to produce written descriptions (a.k.a. think-alouds) of how you're solving the question. In real time. Step by step. It's a time-consuming strategy but hell yes, it works wonders. Before we analyze an example, let me outline the steps that usually help me find the correct answer.

1 Analyze the question

First of all, carefully read the question and highlight, underline or circle keywords. Make sure you really understand what the question is talking about and asking for. If needed, re-read it a second time. Most mistakes are made when you misread the question.

2 Analyze and evaluate the data

Study all the graphs, tables, bar charts, illustrations, passages, etc. given in the question. Highlight key points in these visual representations. Notice the patterns, relationships, and trends. Can you relate them or explain them using your biology understanding?

3 Predict the answer

Before looking at the options given, use your logic and biological knowledge to predict the possible answer. Yes, you heard it right: Read the question → predict the answer → look at the options given. When you're reading the question, identify what possible biological concept is being tested. Then, retrieve basic facts and concepts about that topic from your hippocampus. When you have an anticipated answer, it will be much easier to skim through the options and find the correct answer. In fact, thinking about a possible answer before looking at the options will excite your neurons and challenge your comprehension.

4 Find evidence for the answer options

Check evidence for every single multiple-choice option by:

i. Applying learned concepts and facts. Use your biology knowledge only and not your personal opinion or biased assumptions (for example, that humans evolved from chimps which isn't the case because although chimps may be our closest living relative, we didn't evolve from *them* per se). These scientific facts can be supporting or contradicting to the options given. Always always always try to figure out what concept is being tested in the question as this will point you to the right answer.

ii. Looking at the data given and finding evidence for each statement. Don't just assume, but find correct data to rule out or accept the statement. If you can't, then the statement is invalid. Moreover, to rule out incorrect options you can use the tips outlined in the section titled 'Test Taking Techniques'.

iii. Raising questions *What? How? Why? Are there any alternatives?* Be critical about what you read and see. Also, be open-minded to thinking holistically.

5 Make the decision

This is the easiest part. By the time you reach this point, you should understand what the question is all about, what each illustration means, what concepts are being tested, and what each option refers to. Assimilate all of the evidence, weigh each statement against the others if it's an MCQ, or individually if it's a True/False question, and finally come to the decision. Be careful if the question is asking to select just one answer or several.

So now let's take a look at one example of how to use think-alouds and the steps mentioned above to solve biological problems.

A newly discovered species of frogs, Biologicus olympiadicus, is found widely dispersed in different habitats around the world. Two forms are particularly common - tropical and mediterranean. Examine the pictures of the two frog forms on the right and the data in **Table** *2. What conclusion can you draw using the data given?*

MEDITERRANEAN   TROPICAL

Table 2 Proportions Of Tropical, Mediterranean And Hybrid Frogs Found In Traps

Year	Total	Tropical	Mediterranean	Hybrids
1	1023	0.48	0.50	0.018
2	899	0.48	0.50	0.019
3	905	0.50	0.49	0.009

A. Based on the phylogenetic species concept, tropical and mediterranean frogs are the same species.

B. Based on the morphological species concept, tropical and mediterranean frogs are the same species.

C. Based on the ecological species concept, tropical and mediterranean frogs are different species.

D. Based on the biological species concept, tropical and mediterranean frogs are different species.

E. More information is needed to draw conclusions about the relationship between these two types of frogs.

Now, write down every single step of your thinking. Below is the example of my written think-aloud.

I read the question and highlight key words (which are *'widely dispersed'*, *'different habitats'*, *'tropical'*, *'mediterranean'*, and *'proportions'* from the table title).

Now, I analyze the illustration and look carefully at the external appearance of the frogs. Although they look really similar, there are some differences (e.g., different streak color and number, unequal body size). I don't have any clues about the diet, predators, competitors or any other characteristic of a niche for each species (I only know that they have different habitats). There is no information about their evolutionary relationships. *Attention!* It's important to note down what information is actually lacking, too.

The data in the table shows that there is a constant number of mediterranean and tropical frogs over the three-year period. A much smaller number of hybrids is also found from year 1 to 3. It's not indicated whether these hybrids are viable or fertile.

I am predicting that the correct answer will be the one which is rather vague as I don't have much evidence about the relatedness of the two frogs.

Now I skim through the options and apply my biology knowledge. Since I don't have any information about specifics of ecological niches, I'll rule out C. Since I lack information about frog phylogenetics, common ancestors, and genetic similarity, I'll rule out A. I'll rule out B because I identified some morphological difference between frogs. For D, I need any information about the viability and fertility of hybrids because the biological species concept states that two organisms that have the potential to interbreed in nature and produce viable, fertile offspring, but don't produce viable, fertile offspring with members of other such groups are considered to be the same species. I don't have this information, so I choose E.

What I just did encompasses metacognition, which means thinking about how you're thinking. See, describing and ordering your thought processes is a powerful way to investigate how your brain works. Plus, it helps you identify the gaps where you need to improve your problem solving. And ultimately, these written think-alouds can help you tailor your perfect problem solving strategy. Hey, just keep in mind that you won't become a good problem solver without deep conceptual understanding (e.g., in the question with frogs above, I used my biology knowledge about the different definitions of species) so keep up with your reading and build your tower of knowledge. Every day. For the rest of your life. Oh, and below I put together a small list of common errors and tips how to avoid them that you can use as a skeleton for developing your problem solving strategy.

Common Errors In Problem Solving

Now that you have some clues about how to approach problem solving, it's time to look at another good way to learn to solve problems. And again, you know this one! It's learning from your mistakes. Obvious, no? So, I've summarized the most common mistakes I made when solving problems in **Table 3**. Most will be familiar to you, so pay attention and learn from them.

Table 3 Most Common Problem Solving Mistakes And How To Avoid Them

Mistake	Explanation	How to avoid it?
Disregarding evidence and data in the question	Sometimes we don't use some or all of the information provided in the question.	Study thoroughly all the data provided. Highlight keywords and key parts of the tables, charts, and figures. Don't forget the legends.
Misreading	Due to tight time limits and stress in the olympiad, we usually read the question or the answer options incorrectly.	Highlight, circle, or underline the key parts of the question and options as you read to avoid misreading.
Answering the question based on opinion	We tend to base our answer on an opinion or biased assumption and not on biology knowledge.	Find supporting evidence for the option from your biology knowledge (or from data given) and suppress your urge to use your own opinion.
Making incorrect assumptions about data	We may misinterpret the graphs and data given to us.	Highlight the numbers, use a ruler, circle or mark the points in the tables or graphs. Understand the trends and the possible reasons for why numbers go up or down or stay the same.
Failure to apply biology knowledge	We may have an incorrect or incomplete understanding of biology content as we didn't absorb enough information or misinterpreted information.	Make sure you read and study many biology textbooks and build a good, in-depth understanding of different biology topics and concepts. Ask teachers or find a tutor to help you get the hang of the things you don't get.
Select the option without any rationale	Sometimes we use gut feeling to choose the correct answer. We don't bother to find explanations for the options and just select something that appears to be logical.	Avoid making decisions based on a gut feeling or because that particular option just feels right. Support every single option with evidence based on biological concepts. You can also scribble the explanation next to the option or just say it in your mind. If you can't find an explanation, most likely that option is false.

Problem Solving Questions

So far, you've learned about the steps involved in problem solving and key mistakes we usually make. Apart from that, you need to understand what types of questions you can expect to get in the biology olympiad. How? By doing past papers to familiarize yourself with the format of the questions (that's the reason why I always advise students to do past papers *before* they even start reading any biology textbook).

You might have heard of the Bloom's Taxonomy [26], which is typically used to assess the level of questions in different biology olympiads. For example, the USABO Semifinal Part A consists of multiple-choice questions approximately equally distributed among the three areas of lower cognition (~60 – 70% of total) and questions testing the higher levels of cognition, primarily analysis with some synthesis and evaluation (~40 – 30% of the total) [27]. In contrast, Part B focuses primarily on Bloom's higher level of cognition (~70 – 80%) with some questions testing your lower cognition (~30 – 20%). The Bloom's Taxonomy is also widely used to assess the Medical College Admission Test (MCAT), the Bio-Medical Admissions Test (BMAT), Graduate Record Examinations (GRE), and Advanced Placement (AP) biology exams. But what the hell do all of these lower and higher levels of cognition mean?

Well, according to this tool, six different levels are used to categorize your thinking. Take a look at **Table 4** where I summarized the different levels and their biological examples. Note that **analysis, synthesis**, and **evaluation** are true higher-order cognitive skills which require the application of knowledge and critical thinking (all of which are tested in the olympiad). Thus, you can expect to see a lot of questions that fall into those three categories.

Table 4 Bloom's Taxonomy and Examples

Level	Description	Example
Knowledge	Questions involve **rote memorization** and **recall** of biology concepts and facts.	*Which organelle is important for protein degradation?* *A. Ribosomes* *B. Proteasomes* *C. Ubiquitin* *D. Golgi apparatus* *E. Rough endoplasmic reticulum* To answer the question, you just need to know that proteasomes (answer is B) are big molecular machines that shred ubiquitinated proteins. There is no thinking involved here, just retrieval of the information.

Comprehension

Questions require **understanding** of biological concepts and they test your ability to extrapolate and interpret information.

Which of the following statements correctly describes why the intensity of the bands on a Northern blot are different in lane A and lane B? Note the marker is shown in lane M.

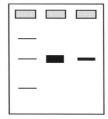

A. *In lane A, RNA is most likely supercoiled whereas in lane B it is mostly linear.*

B. *In lane A, more labelled antibody probe was added, which shows a greater signal.*

C. *Probe concentration was too high in lane A compared to lane B.*

D. *The concentration of agarose is different between lane A and B.*

E. *In lane A, RNA expression was greater than in lane B.*

This question is testing your understanding of the gel and how it works. It tests whether you understand that the band darkness depends on how much of the molecule of interest you've got.

Statement A is false because supercoiled means that surface area of the molecule is much lower and therefore the molecule would move faster than a linear molecule so gel bands will be at different heights. B is false because in a Northern blot we use single stranded nucleic acid probes, not antibodies.
C is false because there is a washing step in the procedure which removes excess unbound probe molecules.
D is false because lanes A and B are on the same gel, meaning that agarose concentration should be uniform across the entire gel.
E is the correct statement because the Northern blot enables us to see *how much* mRNA there is in the sample. The darker the band, the more mRNA was in our sample.

Application	Questions present new concepts and you have to **apply** your knowledge to a new situation.	*Dithiothreitol (DTT) is a commonly used chemical that acts as a reducing agent. Which of the following gels (1-5) shows the most likely banding pattern if you analyzed a dimeric protein containing a 40 kDa protein attached to a 15 kDa protein by a disulfide bridge using SDS-PAGE and a very small DTT concentration?*

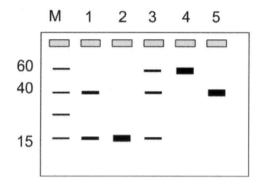

First, remember what SDS-PAGE is used for. It allows you to separate proteins based on the size, but not charge (knowledge). Now, if you have a native dimeric protein, its size will be 55 kDa. If it was denatured, you would see two bands of 40 kDa and 15 kDa (comprehension). The question said that you add a very **small** concentration of DTT, meaning that it will oxidize some but probably not all disulfide bridges (application). This means you'll have a mixture of denatured and undenatured protein. Answer: 3.

Analysis	Questions involve **interpretation** of data, graphs, charts or figures; **analyzing** a scientific case; and **comparing** and **contrasting** complex information.	*A scientist synthesized a molecule called X. To test its effects on red blood cells (RBCs), he incubated RBCs with and without molecule X for 24 hrs. Using the oxygen dissociation graph below, decide which of the following statements is correct. Select all that apply.*

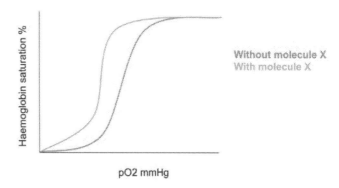

A. At the same partial pressure of O_2, the saturation of hemoglobin without molecule X will be higher than the saturation of hemoglobin with molecule X.

B. The graph of hemoglobin without molecule X will exhibit cooperativity.

C. The graph with molecule X shows the features of fetal hemoglobin whereas the red graph shows normal adult oxygen dissociation curve.

D. Mammals adapted to high altitude would benefit from the treatment with molecule X.

E. If 2,3-BPG was added, both graphs would shift towards the left.

Statement A is false because you can see that the purple graph is always higher than the red graph, meaning that without molecule X, the saturation of hemoglobin is lower. B is correct because cooperative behavior exhibits a sigmoidal curve. C is true because you can see that the purple graph is shifted to the left, meaning there is a greater affinity for oxygen. In the fetus, RBCs have to extract as much oxygen from the mother as possible and thus hemoglobin must have a much higher affinity compared to adult hemoglobin. D is true because at high altitude, oxygen is scarce. This means that hemoglobin must have a higher than normal affinity to take up as much oxygen from the atmosphere as possible.

E is false because 2,3-BPG triggers more oxygen to be unloaded to different tissues from hemoglobin. So the graph would shift towards the right (a.k.a. Bohr shift), not the left.

| **Synthesis** | You analyze given information, **develop** a hypothesis, **design** an experiment or **create** a model about a particular biological phenomenon. | *A newly discovered species of crickets lives on the small cactus plant and feeds on nectar which the cactus produces at the tips of spines. Which of the following experiments is the most useful to test the hypothesis that crickets defend the cactus from leaf-eating bugs?*
 A. Remove leaf-eating bugs and measure the rate of plant growth.
 B. Remove the spines and measure the density of crickets.
 C. Remove the glands that produce nectar and measure the density of crickets.
 D. Remove the crickets and measure the rate of plant growth.
 E. Remove leaf-eating bugs and measure the density of crickets.

 Since the question is asking about the effects of crickets on defense against leaf-eating bugs, your experiment should focus on investigating what would happen if you remove the crickets and how this would affect plant growth. If crickets protect the plant, you would see a decrease in plant growth. If crickets don't have any effect, then there will be no difference in plant growth. And if crickets have a negative effect, plant growth would increase when you remove them. Thus, the answer is D. |
| **Evaluation** | Questions will make you **critique** an experiment, its design or a given biological case. You will have to **appraise** data in support of a hypothesis and **assess** given conclusions. | *A blue pigment called phycocyanin is extracted from a marine alga. Which of the following statements best supports the hypothesis that the pigment is important for photosynthesis? Phycocyanin:*
 A. is found in land algae and land plants that carry out photosynthesis.
 B. has magnesium like chlorophyll a.
 C. has a molecular conformation that mimics chlorophyll a.
 D. is highly abundant in chloroplasts, the site of photosynthesis.
 E. has an absorption spectrum that resembles the action spectrum of photosynthesis.

 You need to compare different statements and assess how they contribute to the hypothesis. Of the options given, only E truly provides evidence between structure and function, i.e. the absorption spectrum of a pigment |

matches the action spectrum, meaning it's involved in photosynthesis. A-D may all be correct as statements, however, they don't show any links between phycocyanin on photosynthesis. For instance, if you look at statement A, many other pigments are found both in algae and plants, but this does not mean that those pigments specifically function in photosynthesis.

How To Study To Develop Thinking Skills

Now that you know what different olympiad problems may be testing you on, it's time to modify your study habits to prepare yourself for those tricky problem solving questions. Crowe *et al.* created what is called the Bloom's-based Learning Activities for Students (BLASt) [28]. It's a powerful and indispensable tool designed to strengthen your study skills at each level of the Bloom's Taxonomy and it's really useful for your biology olympiad preparation, too. Check **Table 5** out to get familiar with many suggestions of different learning activities.

Table 5 Learning Activities For Students (Blast) Who Are Preparing For The Biology Olympiad

Level	How to study?
Knowledge	Read as many biology textbooks as you can
	Make mind maps
	Use flashcards
	Do topic-wise worksheets, end-of-chapter questions
	Analyze past olympiad papers
	Quiz yourself on key terms, definitions, and vocabulary
	Take notes
	Prepare presentations
	Draw and label diagrams
	Watch explanatory videos
	Attend school biology lessons
	Sign up for summer camps in the university
	Do an online undergraduate biology course
	Join a school science club

Comprehension	Summarize biological concepts, laws, ideas, and processes in your own words when taking notes (don't copy-paste)
	Teach others, e.g., in a science club
	Practice writing mini paragraphs using a biological word or phrase, e.g., a paragraph summarizing how you understand natural selection
	Have examples in your head for all key concepts, e.g., of sympatric speciation or directional selection
Application	When revising, raise such questions: What would happen if you increased or decreased this or that? What would happen if you add/remove this or that?
	Make graphs, biochemical pathways, and negative feedback schemas to understand how one component affects others
Analysis	Get past papers, look for university-level biology problems online, or download some published scientific papers (see a subsection below with more sources). Analyze and interpret data in the graphs, tables, charts and figures
	Analyze a question, compare and contrast statements, and relate data to the arguments
Synthesis	Identify a question or uncertainty and propose a hypothesis or design an experiment to test it
	Create a map of facts and concepts or a model to explain relationships, e.g. from the information about mutant strains of bacteria, recreate the biochemical pathway with its intermediates and enzymes
Evaluation	Google some experiment examples and assess the strengths and weaknesses of the experiment in writing, paying attention to:
	Variables (independent, dependent, and controlled)
	• Are there positive and negative control groups? Are they set up correctly?
	• Are the factors/subjects in the experimental group appropriate?
	• Were the experimental results achieved by taking precise measurements?
	• Can the results be replicated with the same results over and over again?
	• What are the possible sources of error that may have skewed the experiment results? Were they controlled or reduced?
	Assess the limitations of different experimental approaches.
	Evaluate if the data supports the hypothesis.

Where To Find Problem-solving Questions For Practice

The Medical College Admission Test (MCAT), the Graduate Record Examination (GRE) Biology practice test, IBO past papers, past papers of different biology olympiads in English (or any other language that you understand), MIT OpenCourseWare exams and assessments, International Baccalaureate (IB) Biology, Advanced Placement (AP) Biology, and A-Level Biology papers are all good resources to develop your problem solving skills. On Biolympiads.com you will also find different worksheets and question banks for practicing. Work on problem solving questions on a regular basis using the tips from this section and I hope that soon you'll refine your sparkling problem solving strategy which will guide you through the biology olympiad.

In the next section, I'll share my top-notch tips on how to answer the questions in the olympiad if you haven't got a clue what they're talking about.

15 TEST TAKING TECHNIQUES

> *"Genius is one percent inspiration and ninety-nine percent perspiration."*
> *Thomas Edison*

In many biology olympiads worldwide and some other exams such as medical admission tests (Medical College Admission Test (MCAT) in the USA and the BioMedical Admissions Test (BMAT) and UK Clinical Aptitude Test (UKCAT) in the UK), you'll come across mainly multiple choice questions (MCQs). The reason why they're so popular is that an MCQ test measures various kinds of knowledge, including understanding of terminology, facts, concepts, principles, and scientific procedures as well as your ability to apply and interpret biological knowledge. There are different types of MCQs and you need to be able to distinguish between them as this will help you answer the question correctly.

By far the most common type is a single correct answer question where all but one of the choices are incorrect. These best answer questions are one of the hardest, as the alternatives are all essentially correct but differ in their degree of correctness. You need to be able to distinguish the option that is clearly *more* correct than the others. In negative MCQs, you'll have to identify the alternative that is false, or sometimes the alternative that is the *worst* answer of all the given options. Multiple response questions (a.k.a. 'Select all that apply' type of questions) have more than one correct answer. Combined response questions ask you to select the correct answer or answers by choosing one of a set of letters, each of which represent a combination of different alternatives.

For all of these types of questions, there are different ways of scoring. Some can be scored on an all-or-none basis, where one point is given if all the correct answers are selected and zero points are given if there is at least one incorrect statement selected. In some olympiads, each alternative is scored independently: one point for each correct answer or (1 point)/(total number of statements) points for each correct answer chosen. Sometimes scoring can be based on the following distribution: 4 correct responses = 1 point, 3 = 0.6, 2 = 0.2, and 1 or 0 = 0.

But that's not the full story.

As you may have noticed already, the olympiad now combines MCQs and true-false questions. Although I previously said that the biology olympiad is all about testing your understanding, you can boost your score despite the fact that you may not have any clue about solving problems. Wondering how? I put together a list of reliable strategies for answering the olympiad questions correctly. Applying tips and tricks from this section alone won't guarantee qualifying for the next round of the competition. But it'll certainly help you *improve* your test taking strategy.

Depending on the type of the question, one trick might be more suitable than others. Occasionally, tips described here won't be applicable at all - this depends on the context of the question. So, in the exam, keep your mind open and be critical with regards to what the question is asking for. Let's go!

1 Pay attention to the point value

Some questions are worth 1 point and some are worth 2 points. Sometimes there could be an indication that there will be 0.25 points given for each correct statement. Pay attention to the point value of the question and instructions like, *'Select all that apply'*, *'Select two best answers'*, *'Select the best statement'*, *'Which of the following statements are correct'*, *'Which of the following statements is correct'*, etc. Sometimes you answer incorrect because you failed to spot that the question asked for more than one correct answer. So be careful and always underline or circle those key words which indicate how many answers you should choose.

Also, train yourself to circle or underline words like *'false'*, *'incorrect'*, *'correct'*, or *'true'*. Have you ever selected the wrong answer just because you didn't pay attention to exactly what the question was asking for? Also, watch out for double negatives like *'isn't incorrect'*, *'not uncommon'*, *'not insignificant'*, etc. How do you deal with them? Rephrase the negatives so that the question or option makes sense to you. For example, *'not uncommon'* can be rephrased to *'widespread'*.

2 Always use a highlighter

A highlighter is a fluorescent probe in the question. It helps you spot that particular word(s) and select the correct answer. Mark *only* the key information – there is no need to highlight everything, got it? Usually, one to three words, including an adjective, a verb, or a noun, is enough. Note that it's bad practice to highlight whole sentences or paragraphs. What I mean is, too much is just as bad as too little.

3 If there are two opposing answers, pick one or the other

When you come across two opposing statements, it usually means that one of the options will be the correct one. Why? Usually, opposing statements can't both be correct or incorrect at the same time. However, you need to be cautious here as this rule isn't globally applicable. There are cases where you have opposing statements but it isn't about choosing one or the other because both are wrong scientifically. For instance, imagine a question about restriction digestion with restriction enzymes.

What would happen to the shape of the DNA if you cut a plasmid with a restriction enzyme?

A. Linear to supercoiled.
B. Nicked to linear.
C. Nicked to supercoiled.
D. Supercoiled to linear.
E. Supercoiled to nicked.

See, A. and D. are opposing and E. and C. are opposing. Scientifically speaking, plasmids are circular so an option that starts with supercoiled will be correct. If you add a restriction enzyme, it cuts both the top and bottom strands, linearizing the molecule. The answer will thus be D.

4 Don't pick an answer which is too simple or obvious

In olympiad papers, there are many tricky questions that seem quite easy and, more importantly, obvious. Intuitively, you may choose the simplest answer. But here's the rub. Don't trust your gut too often! Before choosing an answer, remember that you're in the biology olympiad, not in a simple school exam. Olympiad papers are designed to stretch and challenge you and your brain. Let's get to the point - the simplest answer won't be correct in many cases. Make sure you know why you're choosing a particular answer and don't just rely on your sixth sense.

5 Never leave blank answers

Pretty obvious, no? But I've heard so many stories from students who were so stressed out during the last few minutes of the test that they didn't even put any guesses on the answer sheet. At the beginning of the test, if you don't know the answer to the question, skip it and come back later. Always leave 5-10 minutes at the end of the test to make educated guesses. There is still a 20% chance (1 out of 5) that you might be correct. It goes without saying that leaving a question blank guarantees no points whatsoever. Wanna hear the good news? If you apply some of the tips from this list, you can actually increase your chance of guessing a correct answer by up to 50%.

6 If the question is very long, read only the last sentence of the question

For very long questions, read the last sentence of the question first - this is usually the statement that ends in a question mark. Try to select the answer using only the information from that last sentence. If something is unclear, only then do you go back and read the entire question.

This skill takes a lot of time to practice since in schools we're always taught to first read and analyze the question carefully (sometimes teachers say to read it twice!), and only then move to the answer options. But hey, when you read the question first, you can become quite biased, or even confused, no?! All the little details, unknown words, and convoluted sentences in the long chunky paragraph are there to muddle you. Intentionally. Cunningly. So don't get caught in those traps. How? Do past papers at home with a timer, using the LAST QUESTION SENTENCE → ANSWER OPTIONS → WHOLE QUESTION order to read long questions. *Nota bene*! This applies only to *long* questions. There is no need to read answers first for short questions - this won't save you much time.

7 Start the paper from the end

Counterintuitive, right? This is what I call a bottom-up test taking technique, which means you start with the *hardest* questions first. Are you asking why? Well, at the beginning of the test your brain (and eyes) still are fully concentrated on the task. Don't waste your mental power on easy questions. Instead, leave the easy ones for dessert, when you'll probably be knackered! Again, to master this skill you need to (re)train yourself under *timed* conditions by doing past olympiad papers starting with the last page of the exam. You won't regret it. Promise.

Also, if your exam is comprised of Part A and B, I would recommend doing Part B first as it's usually the hardest one. If the exam is comprised of Part A, Part B, and Part C as in the USABO semifinals, start with Part B, then do Part A and finish with Part C. This is because Part B is the most mentally demanding so you want to do it first when your mind is very sharp. Part A can give you some easy points so do it next. Although you'll be a bit tired after Part B, easy points will boost your morale. Then, go to Part C which has a varying number of points (i.e. the more correct answers you provide, the more points you get). So after you did Part A and B, you can spend the remaining time writing down as many facts as you can for Part C.

8 Pay attention to vague key words and absolutes

Sometimes, olympiad questions are ridiculously easy but many students (myself included) fail to spot the correct answer because we don't pay attention to keywords. Be wary of these words, which include MUST, HAS TO, ALWAYS, NONE, NEVER, ONLY, ALL, ENTIRE, MOST, ANY, EVERYTHING, NO MATTER, NOTHING, IMPOSSIBLE, etc., which indicate the absence of any exceptions. Sloppy reading can be particularly disastrous with items such as these. Instead, in the options always look for relative (flexible) words like OFTEN, USUALLY, SEEM, MIGHT, and MAY, which indicate that the statement is correct. Bear in mind that biology is a subject that doesn't conform to conventional rules. It is filled with marvellous exceptions and so sentences full of extremes are rarely correct.

9 Master the diagrams from biology textbooks

There are many awesome textbooks to help you prepare for the olympiad. You need to be able to recall the diagrams, graphs, and cross-sections of animal and plant anatomy and histology. No, I'm not kidding. Have a look at the past papers and you'll find a myria(po)d (only biologists will get this zoo(il)logical joke!) of questions that were based on diagrams. Don't forget phylogenetic trees. Although biosystematics make up only 5% of the test, sometimes those additional two or three points are all you need to get to the next round.

10 Be aware of the general "rules of thumb"

One of the most common 'rules of thumb' is to select the longest answer. This isn't the case in the biology olympiad exam, at least not always. Sometimes these long answers seem really scientifically correct solely because of the bulk of detail in them, tempting you to choose it. But again, that's just a trap for you.

Rumor has it that correct answers are more likely to ring familiar. Exam makers use this 'rule' to create incorrect statements. It may be that you were exposed to a very similar answer once but now one or a few words were changed to give it an incorrect meaning. Don't use your faint sense of déjàvu in the olympiad. The moral of the story: Familiar ≠ Correct.

Another common 'rule of thumb' among students is that, when in doubt, you should choose statement 'C' as your guess. Not so fast! In reality, this isn't a good strategy, since in the majority of cases, you can look for keywords or special, vague words such as *'all'*, *'none'*, and *'always'*, which will indicate if a statement is true or false. So you can often narrow down the options. Let me give you some more evidence. One day I was as bored as the promoter without RNA polymerase so I decided to see whether there is a particular option (A, B, C, D, or E) that is more prevalent than the others in the USABO exams. I looked at all answer keys from USABO 2011-2016 Open exam papers and tallied up how many times each option came up in the exam. These are the averages of correct answer options from 2011-2016 for each possibility:

A - 9   B - 12   C - 12   D - 10   E - 9

Thus, almost all options are equally possible (sorry, I didn't bother to calculate Chi square values and compare them with p values). All in all, don't always stick to option C unless you have a well thought-out reason.

11 Don't forget the units

A very important point in the biology olympiad is to put the units after any numbers or calculations. This holds true not only for biology olympiads, but for mathematics, physics, chemistry, and other subjects. It doesn't take a rocket scientist to realize that you should work in a neat and organized way. Never leave only the answer (especially without the units) without any worked solutions. Show how you came up with the solution and you might even get some extra points!

12 Spend 75% of time doing the questions and 25% checking your answers

In the first ¾ of the exam, flick through all of the questions and try to answer as many as your knowledge allows you to do (don't forget to start from the end and move your way to the first page). Try to make an educated guess if you don't know something. Don't waste time laboring over troublesome questions and leave them for now. Then, for the last half hour, review all the answers you put down to check that you didn't make any accidental silly mistakes. Also, carefully check your answer sheet to make sure you didn't skip a question.

13 Beware of changing your answer

From my personal experience, I can say that the first guess is usually the correct one. How many times have you changed an answer just to find out that your first guess was actually correct? Painful, no? Change your answers, but only if you have a really sound reason for doing so. If you have any doubts, leave it as it is and you'll probably get it right.

14 Skip it

I can't emphasize more that if you reach a difficult question, don't spend a ton of time on it. Leave it and move on. Just flag it on the answer sheet. If you let yourself get bogged down, you might waste too much time and lose a lot of points. Remember, the olympiad is all about two things: (1) critically analyzing the questions and (2) managing your time in order to answer as many questions as possible.

Keep an eye on the time throughout the exam and allocate enough time to answer as many questions as possible.

15 Take a break

If the test is around one hour long, take a short three-minute break in the middle. Eat a sweet, exercise your eyes by squeezing them tightly 10-15 times, or simply extend your leg muscles. Honestly! The break will help you recover and bring fresh blood with oxygen and nutrients to your ravenous photoreceptors and neurons. If the test is between 1.5 and 2 hours, take two breaks of around three to five minutes. During one of them, go to the bathroom where you can jump around, raise your heart rate and make those cardiomyocytes beat faster - you'll soon feel much more refreshed because of a rush of adrenaline in your arteries!

16 Know your basic chemistry well

Although the biology olympiad is about biology and chemistry shouldn't be tested on, hey-ho, reality is different. Biology overlaps with many other subjects, including chemistry, so grab general chemistry and biochemistry textbooks to learn more about these subjects. Oh, and don't ditch the school chemistry course. It'll greatly help you in solving olympiad questions.

17 Know your basic physics well

I highly recommend skimming through a general physics textbook as there are questions in past papers that require you to have a basic understanding of physics and its laws. *Warning*: no need to cover quantum physics or mechanics or anything for the level of the International Physics Olympiad (IPhO). Instead, pay particular attention to the basics of these topics:

- Forces and Newton's laws of motion
- Work and energy
- Fluids
- Thermodynamics
- Electric charge, field, and potential

Also, review common formulas as you need to know the relationship between variables and their application to biological systems (especially in terms of cardiovascular and respiratory systems).

18 Practice math skills

Yes, you read it correctly. Just like for chemistry and physics, you need to have a solid math foundation. Don't get me wrong - it's not a math olympiad and you don't need to know every single little detail from your math course like combinatorics, Euclidean geometry, or number theories. But mastering calculation skills and knowing how to play with probabilities will help you do well in the biology olympiad paper. Basic statistics, probabilities (e.g., dependent and independent events), Fibonacci series, basics of geometry, trigonometry, arithmetic, numerical computation, and algebra (e.g., the binomial theorem) definitely won't do harm. Let's not forget that ecology and evolutionary biology are fields where math skills are also very widely used.

19 Relax before the test

Stress. Anxiety. Frustration. It happens to the best of us, even the ones with the most talent and highest IQ. A stressed mind can prevent you from retrieving key facts from your memory. And, in the worst case scenario, it can lead to mental burn out. Don't let stress ruin all the awesome hard work you've done so far. Remember that this single biology olympiad isn't the end of the world and no matter what will happen after, you'll have many other - or hopefully at least another - chances like this. Set your mind for success. Don't forget that the exam will be hard for everyone and that you are all trapped in the same lymph node. Jokes aside, to manage stress, go to hang out with your nerd friends, watch TV, go to the gym, go shopping, or just sleep before the olympiad. On the test day, believe in yourself if you truly dedicated enough time and effort to studying. For more tricks how to relieve stress, check section 'Test Anxiety'.

Don't blame me if these tips don't help you as it's still your job to learn and know the basics of biology and key scientific facts! Without knowledge, you won't succeed. Be willing to experiment with strategies mentioned above and implement them doing past papers. You'd better review questions that you got wrong and find out *why* you made a mistake. So what are you waiting for?

16 READING A BIOLOGY TEXTBOOK

"Today a reader, tomorrow a leader."
Margaret Fuller

Have you ever found yourself finishing a chapter from a biology textbook but not remembering a single thing? It's an awful feeling, no? Do you think you're unable to absorb all the information you read? The truth is that we're all perfectly imperfect. While reading a million textbooks would be very useful, there are just too many books and too many things to memorize. And you know your time is extremely limited when it comes to the preparation for the biology olympiad.

Reading a biology textbook efficiently is a skill that you can master quite fast. Just like passively walking through an art gallery won't make you an art expert, passively flicking through the textbook won't help you learn biology. Trying to re-read it millions of times won't help either if you don't have a technique, commitment, and, most crucially, an interest in the subject. It's *how* you read it that matters. Not how often. Or how long. Or how many chapters per day. It's the *quality*, not the quantity. Can you handle it? If yes, below I've summarized my sizzling list of tips on how to boost your reading efficiency in order to absorb as much information as possible.

1 Find a quiet area to study

First and foremost, find a quiet place for reading. It can be anywhere from your attic to the library. You see, when you're fully concentrated, it's much easier for you to endocytose information and digest complex facts and figures quickly. On the contrary, if you're distracted, you won't be able to focus and take in new information.

The phone with your social media on it is a huge excuse to procrastinate and whenever it buzzes with a notification, it triggers what I call a phone jerk reflex (not to be confused with the famous knee jerk reflex). What happens is that whenever a message comes, you reflexively reach out to your phone to check it. For most of us, this habit is very hard to stop. Free yourself from such buzzing and jarring distractions. How? Turn off your notifications or put your phone in airplane mode! Also, turn off your computer to cut off any electronic communication. Seriously, you won't miss much in those few hours and you'll be able to check your emails and messages later. Oh, and don't forget to turn off the radio or your music unless it really helps you focus.

Next, deal with any breathing distractions. I call them the 3 **P**'s: **Pals**, **Parents**, and **Pets**. Make it difficult for these 3 P's to reach you in the first place when you're studying. Inform them that you'll be busy with olympiad preparation and won't be reachable. As for pets, walk and feed your dog or cat or any other pet you've got before you delve into your biology world. Lastly, build up your confidence in saying 'no' to tempting offers and invitations from bipeds. If, however, you need to study somewhere in public I recommend using earplugs. It'll help get you isolated from the outside world and focused only on the material you're reading.

Before you begin, make sure you have all of the materials you need for studying like notebooks, post-it notes, pens, pencils, erasers, a calculator, and ruler. The fewer distractions and interruptions you have, the more efficient your reading will be.

2 Review the headings and boldfaced words first

Before you even start reading the chapter, review and familiarize yourself with the headings and boldfaced words first. This will prime your brain for that specific topic and switch on those neurons that already know a bit about that particular topic. When you read the whole chapter, you'll be adding new information to what you already know. To your surprise, your brain will pick out those new facts much easier because it'll anticipate what you're going to read next.

3 Highlight, circle, and underline key words and concepts

For this tip, I highly recommend buying your own textbook copy or using software that allows you to highlight on PDFs. Engage actively with reading. As you read, underline key ideas and write on the margins. Do you remember why Harry Potter's Potions book was successful in *The Half-Blood Prince*? Well, duh! Writing on the margins will help you connect the stuff you're reading to the facts you already know, making it simple for your neurons to solidify what you've just learned. And it'll also help you during revision to find only the parts that you want to review.

I wouldn't recommend taking notes when reading the chapter for the first time. And I have a legitimate reason for that. Wanna hear? If you start taking notes without even knowing what will come up next, do you think the first sentences are worth noting down? Probably not as you most likely need to skim through the next few sentences and then come back. So keep highlighting the key points but don't stop to rewrite things to your notes just yet (see the next tip and you'll understand the whole idea).

4 Read a chapter three times

During the first reading, just skim through the text, note words in bold, and focus on getting a broad understanding of the topic. This will prime your brain for memorization when you read the same chapter again.

As you read the text a second time, it's now a good time to take notes, make diagrams, and mind maps. This will help you comprehend and memorize biology concepts better because you are homogenizing kinesthetic and visual cues in your brainy centrifuge. Besides that, if you make good notes, you may never need to refer back to the book. A little advice: when you're summarizing what you've read, read at least one complete paragraph or the whole section before stopping to write things down into your notes. This will enable you to selectively pick only the most important details from that page. In other words, don't take notes as you read but read more before making a summary.

In your third time, master the concepts. This is when you memorize them using your notes and the textbook. Sound complicated? Indeed, it's the hardest and longest part of reading the textbook. Put a lot of effort into absorbing information because this will determine how well you'll remember information later. And… Again… Utilize different senses to consolidate everything you're learning. Watch biology videos about that topic on the Internet, listen to lectures online, and do practice questions relevant to what you're memorizing. See a section titled 'Memorization Techniques' for more tips on how to remember better.

5 Glance over charts, figures, and tables

Yes, for the biology olympiad you need to know all the diagrams outlined in the key textbooks. And it really isn't that hard to memorize them. Easier said than done, but if you copy them into your notes, you'll be able to carry them around instead of a heavy 1000-page textbook. Whenever you've got a spare minute, glance over the diagrams and soon you'll just know them by heart. Alternatively, get some white sheets of paper (better if it's A3), then draw different biological diagrams on them and hang them in your room. Throughout the day, keep reviewing all the details of the diagrams to accelerate your learning.

6 Read different texts about the same topic

Studying from the same textbook for a long time might make you tired, bored, or frustrated, no? What's worse, you might lose an interest in the subject. Thus, for the sake of change I recommend using at least two different textbooks for the same topic. This will give you a more comprehensive overview of the topic. Plus you'll encounter similar information *again* but only in different words, helping you retain that information better. It'll also make your studying more interesting as you'll be exposed to different pictures, figures, and diagrams.

7 Give yourself short breaks and rewards

When you're reading for a long time, schedule regular 15-minute breaks at the end of each block of 90 minutes of studying. Engage in some activities to warm up your muscles: stretch your legs, arms, and back muscles or go for a short walk/run. I'm guessing you know the benefits of exercise already.

When you complete a reading task, it's time for some teeny-tiny rewards. Treat yourself with something that brings pleasure. Just knowing that after reading a chapter you'll get your deserved reward will keep you motivated to pursue your goals, won't it?

8 Don't ignore the end-of-chapter summaries

After you finish reading the entire chapter, skim through the end-of-chapter summary to recap all the details you learnt. Buddy, remember that repetition is tantalizingly effective. You can also read the end-of-chapter summary for the chapter you read yesterday before you delve into the next chapter to review all that you learnt the previous day.

9 Use audio books

Many biology textbooks are now sold as audio books. These might be super helpful when you're knackered after a long day at school. Or when you couldn't be bothered to read. *Attention*! If you try to multi-task (say you're exercising at the same time as you're listening to the audio), your learning may stall. Why? Simply because your brain now has to do two jobs at the same time instead of one. This means your focus for every particular task is reduced. So to get all of the benefits of the audio book, jump on your couch, relax, and turn on your audio player. At the same time, you can also take notes on what you hear to further stimulate memory consolidation.

10 Discuss what you read with your peers

There is no better way to learn than by teaching others and sharing your knowledge with your peers or family members. When you're teaching others, you're intensely processing information you learnt from your biology textbooks with the goal of making it understandable for everyone. This, in turn, creates some long lasting memories in your brain. So pack your textbooks and go and meet your friends. From time to time. Not too often. Have a plan for the meeting and try to avoid discussing other irrelevant things like the upcoming football match or relationships with boyfriends/girlfriends. Remember, the meeting is solely for educational purposes so discuss only what you read and clarify all marvelous scientific uncertainties. Listen attentively and focus maximally during the conversation!

11 Use time-boxing

When you are in the mood of *'Let's get this studying done'*, schedule specific blocks of time for reading and studying biology throughout the day. This strategy will help you stick to your schedule as you'll know specifically when and what to do, in which order, and how long to do it for. For more tips how to do this, go to section 'Time Management'. By setting these daily time boxes, you'll put some time pressure on yourself which will motivate you to work more efficiently and quickly to complete the task on time and move on to the next one. Since you aren't a loser, you'll stick to your reading commitment and complete it, right?

12 Layer your studying

You don't need me to remind you that biology is a complex, information heavy subject. At times, you might feel really overwhelmed by the breadth of the information you need to remember. It's not a secret that in order to succeed in the olympiad, you need to know not only the concepts from the school curriculum, but also at least the first one or two years of the undergraduate biology curriculum. It's soooo frustrating, isn't it?

But... There is a way to deal with it. And it all comes down to this: the 'layering' technique. According to this method, you first set your mind to learn the simplest biology facts and concepts. You'll use this knowledge to form solid foundations in biology before you gradually add more complex details. Layer upon layer. If you utilize this technique, you'll be able to comprehend information better and easier than if you started with an advanced textbook.

Aside from that, you'll be less anxious about the complexity of the subject itself as you'll smoothly transition from less complex information to more complex information. Put simply, don't jump to some advanced biochemistry or molecular biology textbook. First familiarize yourself with the basics of chemistry and cell biology from a general biology book. Then, gradually move to more advanced textbooks and build upon what you already know.

HOW TO PREPARE FOR THE BIOLOGY OLYMPIAD AND SCIENCE COMPETITIONS

13 Surround yourself with a group of insanely motivated people

Remember that I just told you to isolate yourself from all friends, pets, and relatives. You see, sometimes in life we have those gloomy moments where we don't want to do anything anymore and the only thought that is soaring in our neuron-stuffed heads is to give up. During those breakdown moments, you need breathing creatures to motivate you. You heard it right - humans *inspire* humans. Funnily enough, you don't even need to talk to them or hang out with them. For instance, when I'm merely surrounded by hard-working people, I feel empowered and motivated to work harder myself. In fact, it almost feels like I'm competing against them and I definitely don't want to be bringing down the productivity of the entire room. So then I work even harder. More efficiently. More passionately. Wouldn't you do the same? Oh, and before we end this section, I wanted to share the best of the best tip that works well for me (and hopefully for you) which I call **SPAR** - **S**top **P**rocrastinating **A**nd **R**ead.

17 SO WHERE TO START?

> "Do what you can,
> with what you have,
> where you are."
> *Theodore Roosevelt*

Finally! You reached the most important part of the book! And I reckon this is one of the reasons you're reading this book in the first place. Yes, every single student is wondering how to start preparing for the olympiad. I hope all the previous chapters have convinced you that the biology olympiad is a tough nut to crack. But if you're really committed to getting started (and I'm sure you're) then follow these steps to make sure you get the best out of your preparation.

1 Find a syllabus for your national biology olympiad

You see, many biology olympiads are based on a particular curriculum. To be honest, I've never seen one from my country's national biology olympiad, but other countries usually have one. The IBO also published a syllabus that you can access online [29], but how much exam creators use it remains a spooky mystery. If you can't find any syllabi, then use the one from the IBO because, after all, we're all striving to qualify for the international round. So what do you do with the syllabus? Well, an important part of it is about percentage distribution of topics in the exams:

Cell Biology (20%) (including structure and function of cells and their components, microbiology, and biotechnology)

Plant Anatomy and Physiology (15%) (with emphasis on seed plants)

Animal Anatomy and Physiology (25%) (with emphasis on vertebrates and humans)

Ethology (5%)
Genetics and Evolution (20%)
Ecology (10%)
Biosystematics (5%)

Distribute your time and effort according to these percentages. Logically thinking, it wouldn't be wise to study biosystematics from a university-level textbook for six months and spend like a week or so on animal anatomy and physiology. No kidding, allocate enough time to cover the three biggies: Cell Biology, Animal Anatomy and Physiology, and Genetics and Evolution.

2 Create a study schedule that fits your life

Now, this is a big point where I failed terribly. Ouch... When I started preparing for the olympiad, I didn't have any form of strategy for how to approach the preparation. I had no clue what to read, or how often, or from where. Let alone how to plan my limited time. I was studying like crazy from as many books as possible, didn't do any practice worksheets, and only skimmed through the past papers. I skipped school. I didn't go out. But after all of that, I felt quite burned out. Don't get me wrong! I truly enjoyed the entire journey. The only problem was that I didn't have a well-structured plan. And just like a denatured protein without its 3D structure, I wasn't able to function efficiently. As painful as it sounds, I wasted most of my time stuffing my brain with information ineffectively, while I could have learnt the same things in a shorter amount of time if I had had a good strategy and plan.

So listen buddy, you do need to have a strategic approach and a comprehensive roadmap telling you exactly what to do to reach your goal. And you should know exactly what you want to achieve before committing to all the hard work. The secret to having an effective strategy for the olympiad is to create a *personal* timetable (weekly and monthly) that fits *your* commitments and which works for *you* to help *you* reach *your* goal. I couldn't stress more that it must be suitable just for *you*. Not for your friend. Not for your parents. Only for *you*. This plan will get rid of the doubts and insecurities that usually ignite procrastination and it'll also keep you on top of things. *Attention!* As I already mentioned in the section 'Study Plan', don't you dare leave out time for relaxation and recreational activities from your timetable as this will help you stay sane!

3 Do past papers

Many school students are surprisingly resistant (just like bacteria to some antibiotics, no offence!) to the idea of doing past papers. I've got no clue *why*, but probably because they don't feel quite ready to do them. Or perhaps some students may be deterred by a 'bad' score on a past paper and this can make them feel overwhelmed. And when you have that mindset, the last thing you want to do is study biology for any longer. But... Studying without taking past papers is like fishing without bait!

I remember looking at the first papers of my national biology olympiad. Honestly, I was scared stiff. Oh dear... I didn't know a thing in those tests. It was so mind-numbingly hard and the only thing that was spinning in my gyrated cerebral cortex was, "What the hell are they talking about in all of these stupid questions?" Don't fall into these traps of your emotions and mind – the earlier you look at the past papers, the better. How does this work?

Well, you'll know what topics may come up and how deeply you need to know them. Every day that you delay taking the practice exam is a day you'll spend preparing for a biology olympiad exam that you aren't quite familiar with. Honestly, you won't know the types of questions, the structure of the paper, and the depth of knowledge required to succeed in the olympiad. And if you jump on the preparation train without first looking at past papers, you can definitely arrive at the wrong destination, can't you?

Now, I have some important suggestions on how to do the past papers. First, take each past paper under a realistic setting. Set a timer and do the entire test in one go. Don't split it up into several chunks. Managing time to finish the paper in time is a worthwhile skill to develop. And for this you need to practice, practice, and practice.

At this point you shouldn't freak out about your score. If it's good, GREAT! This means you won't have to work as hard because you've already got a solid understanding of what you need to know for the olympiad. If it's bad, GREAT! Think I'm kidding? No way! You've just prevented a terrific disaster from happening in the actual biology olympiad. See, at least now you know exactly what you need to work on, which topics to review, and what skills to develop. So don't mind the bad score and kick start your studying.

Next, when you read the book, pay all your attention to those miniature details and concepts that you came across in the past papers. And when you're done with your reading, it's good to re-do all of the past papers *again* and score yourself to check your progress. Oh, and now make a list of the topics that came up in the exams repeatedly. This will help you find the topics from which *no* question has ever been asked. Thus, you can kind of predict what might come up next year.

Usually, many people tend to use this study dogma for the olympiad preparation:

1 Content review from key biology textbooks
2 Practice problems (a.k.a. topic-wise worksheets)
3 Past papers

Are you using the same one too? What I'd recommend is to shuffle this dogma to the following:

1 Past papers
2 Content review from key biology textbooks
3 Practice problems (a.k.a. topic specific worksheets)
4 Past papers

In this way, you'll know the format and scope of the olympiad before you dive into the ocean of biology textbooks. Also, don't leave the IBO papers for too late since the aim of any national olympiad is to select the four brightest and most talented students to represent their country in the IBO. This means that the format and questions of your national biology olympiad will probably be very similar to that of the IBO.

4 Read the textbooks

In biology you need to memorize a hell of a lot in order to succeed. General principles of physics and common chemical reaction mechanisms which you can apply to almost any situation make physics and chemistry easy subjects to learn for those who have good thinking skills. On the other hand, biology is full of exceptions and what's really annoying is that it has many contradictions. Rarely do biological concepts and laws make sense, so you just need to know them. By heart. Period.

Sound complicated? It really isn't.

Focus on trying to read five chapters a week during the school year. This will get you to around 10-15 hours a week. During holidays, increase your reading load and cover more advanced biology textbooks, and spend around 30-45 hours per week. Start with a general biology textbook to get a broad understanding of all biology topics first. Read through each chapter three times before you move on to the next one (see section 'Reading a Biology Textbook'). This will allow you to absorb the information most effectively. Refer back to the section 'Memorization Techniques' to help you keep the information in your head for longer!

Then, when you have achieved a solid understanding of basic biology, it's time to delve deeper into the subject. The olympiad is about college-level biology so you'll have to work hard to reach the IBO level. Strive to read at least one advanced book for each of the major biology fields, including one for cell biology, plant biology, human physiology and anatomy, and genetics and evolution. It's worth reading at least one book specific to ecology, but remember that this topic makes up only 10% of the exam so don't spend too much time on it. The same applies to phylogenetics and systematics which comprise only 5% of exam questions.

I feel that you're now thinking, "So which books are the best for the biology olympiad?" Let me tell you this straight. There is no one book that is the best for the olympiad. And no, there is no list of the best books that you need to read either (although on Biolympiads.com you'll find a recommended list; it's merely for reference purposes). Listen, just take any new general biology book, any cell biology book, any genetics book, etc. and you'll be fine. Trust me, all books contain almost the same information. Besides don't use books that are more than five years old. Biology is a dynamic field and new things are being discovered literally every single second. And most importantly, it's not about which book you use but about how well you remember what you read.

5 Do topic-specific worksheets

Have you ever noticed that when you have the book in front of you, you think you'll know and remember everything that you've just read? Honestly, you most likely won't recall a single thing the next day. How can you avoid this? Do topic-wise worksheets along the way. It'll be a checkpoint in your study cycle where your progress will be assessed. What's more, mistakes that you make in those practice papers will steer you in the right direction. Also, write down the topics that you are finding hard when doing practice problems. Then, invest some extra time to review them thoroughly until you feel confident in all areas of biology. No matter how much you study for the olympiad, you'll be asked at least one question that you don't know the answer to. So make sure you brush up on the things you have identified as challenging for you.

Additionally, don't forget to find out why you got a question wrong and find your weak spots. Don't just accept the fact that you were wrong. It's all about *why*. Consult your biology teacher, talk to your nerdy friends in the science club, or email people from university to help you understand and solve a question that you're stuck on. Similarly, pay attention to the questions that you guessed correctly. Yep, identify *how* you arrived at the correct answer so that next time you can use the same trick.

6 Study using online resources

There are soooo many good resources online so make sure to use them for your olympiad preparation. Google some nice notes, mind maps, and summaries of complicated topics, or just browse for biology videos and tutorials. All those resources on the Internet are there for you to use. When you get bored with reading the textbook, just watch some lectures instead. It'll do you good, mate. First, your eyes and fingers will have some time to reset. Second, different senses will be engaged allowing you to absorb information using different learning modalities. Third, this will deter boredom as passive reading might significantly decrease your attention levels. So switch between reading and using interactive learning.

7 Don't forget the practical part

I already mentioned that biology is a very hands-on subject. In the IBO, 50% of your score comes from the practical part. Man, this means you need to develop quite a solid foundation of lab skills. Over the years, I've gathered a list of key techniques (lucky you!) that you need to know for the biology olympiad so check the section titled 'Developing Practical Skills' for this list. Some of the techniques are also outlined in the IBO Syllabus [29].

8 Ask students who succeeded for their advice

I'm sure there is at least one person in your school who succeeded in the biology olympiad. If you don't know anyone, join the Biolympiads Study Group (head to www.biolympiads.com) where you'll find many past participants of different biology olympiads from around the world. Connect with them and ask for their olympiad tips and tricks. They clearly know the exam well and can give you first-hand insight into what to expect in the olympiad. Note that these people may already be attending college or university so don't be surprised if they don't respond immediately. Be patient and understanding.

9 Use example questions from as many biology olympiads as possible

Wait what??? Seriously? How can past papers from other olympiads help you prepare for your nationals? You see, every single biology olympiad tests your aptitude, critical, and analytical thinking. So by doing as many papers as you can, you'll not only get theoretical knowledge, but you'll also develop problem solving skills. What's more, you can learn a new language by doing some past papers in the foreign language. For instance, I used to do German and Swiss biology olympiad papers although I am a native Lithuanian speaker. Despite the fact that I never studied German, it was similar enough to English so I didn't struggle that much.

On Biolympiads.com, every year I update exam papers from previous English-speaking biology olympiads, so be sure to take a careful look at them. Trust me, your eyes will start catching the most important key words and patterns of the questions so you'll learn how to find the most correct answer quickly and flawlessly.

10 Practice dealing with stress under competition conditions

Take part in as many *any* kinds of sports or (non)scientific competitions as you can in order to gain experience working under pressure and under tight time limits. In olympiads, or any exams, you'll have a pile of problems to solve and only a few hours to complete them. That's where time management comes in handy. To nail it, sign up for as many biology, chemistry, physics, and other competitions as you can. And listen, it's *not* about winning but about gaining those life-saving skills in managing stress. Oh, and an additional benefit is that those science competitions will help you cement all the stuff you've learnt together. Use it or lose it, as they say.

11 Visualize yourself as a topper

Breathe biology. Sneeze biology. Cry biology. Think biology. Live biology. Be confident mentally. *Never* think you can't. Work hard, dream hard! And, in your own little world, always see yourself as a winner. But don't you dare become arrogant or conceited. There's no need to boast about how good you're (even if you *really* are). Study silently and let your achievements scream instead of your mouth. Eventually, and with a little bit more biological maturity, you'll see that the hard work is paying off. Maybe not today. Not next week. Not next year. Maybe even not for another decade. But at some point, you'll pick the fruits of your hard work. So work up that killer topper's attitude now and set yourself up for a victory!

12 Find a tutor, a.k.a. your inspiration

In a nutshell, find someone who unconditionally believes in *you* and *your* work (you have one fan already ;-} !). Find someone who is *your* inspiration. *Your* motivator. *Your* guide. *Your* biology olympiad icon. It'll rarely be a parent or a close friend. That's why I created a platform, Tutor4Competitions.com, which will connect you with tutors who are past participants of different high school olympiads. I know from my personal experience (and oh well... I didn't have any tutors) that it's difficult to work on your own on things outside of the usual school curriculum. Plus, many teachers have no clue what the biology olympiad entails, let alone how to prepare for it.

Having someone who can help you really makes a huge difference, both academically and mentally. Maybe even more mentally if you find the right person. You see, when you embark on this olympiad ferry, you'll probably balance between staying on the deck and jumping into the cold ocean as it gets harder and harder. So if you have someone you're accountable to, someone who inspires you and guards you from all bad things, like your *p53* gene, you'll stay on the deck until the end.

18 STUDY PLAN

"A good system shortens the road to the goal."
Orison Swett Marden

With the right amount of planning—and many students don't do that—you can successfully complete your revision for the biology olympiad in less time. When you start planning, think about *how*, *when* and *what* you want to revise. The main thing to do is to identify knowledge gaps, select the topics, and design a comprehensive yearly or monthly study plan which will keep you on top of your studying.

Sundays should be your planning day when you set targets for the coming week. This is crucial especially if you're in high school or if you're sitting important exams like A Levels, Advanced Placement (AP), or the International Baccalaureate (IB) exams. Luckily, this process won't take much of your time but will help you stay accountable and focused on your goal. On the planning day, create a study schedule. Just don't be overly ambitious. Life happens and many unexpected things come up all the time. Take into account your personal and academic (other than biology olympiad) commitments. Moreover, set up some rewards (like a tea/coffee break, a phone call to a friend or a physical exercise session). Having these small rewards at various intervals will help you stay motivated and enthused about the journey towards the olympiad.

So there are two different ways for how you can plan your studying. I classify them into topic-specific studying and book-by-book studying. **Table 6** explains the differences between them.

Table 6 Different Types Of Studying For The Biology Olympiad

	Topic-Wise Studying Technique focuses on studying one particular topic at a time from as many books as possible.	Book-By-Book Studying Technique focuses on learning information from only one book at a time.
Pros	You can quickly become an expert in a particular field (e.g. genetics or animal physiology).	You gain a broad overview of all biological topics quicker (i.e. you will be jack of all trades, master of none).
	Might be easier to remember information as you encounter the same facts again and again in different books.	Cost effective as it doesn't require many resources.
	Might be more useful for the olympiad because there is a clear topic distribution in the olympiad (e.g., Cell biology makes 20% and Animal anatomy & physiology makes 25%). You can allocate your efforts accordingly.	May be easier to link different topics together at any time point as you are studying all of them at the same time.
Cons	May be easier to forget the things you learnt a while ago as at any given time point you are focusing on just one very specific field of biology, ignoring others.	You may not have a really comprehensive understanding of any specific topic.
	Requires many resources and different textbooks.	It might be hard to actually memorize information as you are reading new topics all the time without going into too much detail.
	Might take longer as you are reading specialist textbooks that needs more time to review and comprehend.	Might create confusion as none of the topics are covered in greater detail but merely superficially reviewed.

It's completely up to you which method you choose. Grab the one that better suits your lifestyle and learning style. Or try one method one year, and the other the next year. Both have advantages and disadvantages.

I personally combined both methods. Since I started from scratch without having almost any prior biology knowledge, initially I just focused on reading several general biology books and got familiar with a wide range of subjects such as ecology, animal physiology, plants, genetics, and cell biology. Then, the next year I would split my time in blocks and for the next couple of months I would study only cell biology, followed by some months of advanced genetics, then plants, and so on.

It's very crucial to split your time wisely depending on how much time you've got to prepare for the competition. If you've only got a few months left, it isn't a good idea to focus only on one or two topics like animal physiology or plants (i.e. topic-specific learning). It's more worthwhile to review a general biology textbook (i.e. book-by-book learning). In contrast, if you've got a year or more to prepare, start with book-by-book learning and review general biology textbooks first. Then, switch to topic-specific-learning and start specializing in different fields. Always keep in mind that some topics are much more likely to come up than others (for the percentage distribution of different topics, refer to the IBO Guidelines [29]).

Table 7 is an example of a topic-wise study schedule for one year whereas in **Table 9** you will find a comprehensive overview of a study plan with recommended topics and resources for revision. Notice that my recommendation is to start with past papers first, which will give you an understanding of what your biology olympiad is testing and how many details you need to know. In addition, this will act as a diagnostic test which will allow you to identify your current knowledge gaps.

Table 7 One-year Biology Olympiad Study Plan

	WEEK 1	WEEK 2	WEEK 3	WEEK 4
JAN	Past papers	Past papers	Past papers	General biology
FEB	General biology	General biology	General biology	General biology
MAR	General biology	General biology	Biochemistry	Biochemistry
APR	Biochemistry	Biochemistry	Biochemistry	Biochemistry
MAY	Molecular biology & Genetics	Molecular biology & Genetics	Molecular biology & Genetics	Molecular biology & Genetics
JUN	Molecular biology & Genetics	Molecular biology & Genetics	Molecular biology & Genetics	Molecular biology & Genetics
JUL	Plant biology	Plant biology	Plant biology	Plant biology
AUG	Plant biology	Plant biology	Fungi, Protists, Bacteria, Viruses	Animal physiology & Anatomy
SEP	Animal physiology & Anatomy	Animal physiology & Anatomy	Animal physiology & Anatomy	Animal physiology & Anatomy
OCT	Animal physiology & Anatomy	Animal physiology & Anatomy	Animal physiology & Anatomy	Evolution & Phylogenetics
NOV	Evolution & Phylogenetics	Evolution & Phylogenetics	Ethology	Ecology
DEC	Ecology	Practice papers	Practice papers	Practice papers, Past papers

Table 8 shows a proposed weekly study plan for five weeks, which you can use if your olympiad is in one or two months. You can tailor the plan according to your current knowledge and the resources you've got, but remember to revise all topics.

Table 8 Weekly Biology Olympiad Study Plan for 5 Weeks

	SUNDAY	MONDAY	TUESDAY	WEDNESDAY	THURSDAY	FRIDAY	SATURDAY
WEEK 1	Biochemistry	Biochemistry	Biochemistry (worksheets)	Evolution, biodiversity	Evolution, biodiversity	Ecology	Ecology
WEEK 2	Molecular Biology & Genetics	Molecular Biology & Genetics	Molecular Biology & Genetics	Molecular Biology & Genetics (worksheets)	Biochemistry	Biochemistry	Biochemistry
WEEK 3	Plant Biology (Angiosperm Reproduction)	Plant Biology (Plant Responses)	Plant Biology (worksheets)	Plant Biology (worksheets)	Molecular Biology & Genetics	Molecular Biology & Genetics	Molecular Biology & Genetics
WEEK 4	Human Body (Nervous system)	Human Body (Sensory organs)	Human Body (worksheets)	Human Body (worksheets)	Plant Biology (Structure and Development)	Plant Biology (Transport)	Plant Biology (Soil and Plant Nutrition)
WEEK 5	Human Body (Introduction to animal body)	Human Body (Digestive system)	Human Body (Cardiovascular system)	Human Body (Respiratory system)	Human Body (Endocrine system)	Human Body (Immune system)	Human Body (Reproductive system and Development)

Now, you might be asking when you should start preparing for olympiad. It goes without saying that starting in 8th or 9th grade is the best time. You see, you'll have at least four to five years to prepare. And the later you start, the less time you have left.

Table 9 Comprehensive Biology Olympiad Study Plan
Note that the key textbook for Week 1-Week 9 is Campbell Biology.

	MONDAY	TUESDAY	WEDNESDAY	THURSDAY	FRIDAY	SATURDAY	SUNDAY
WEEK 1	National Biology Olympiad Past papers 2005-2007	National Biology Olympiad Past papers 2008-2010	Rest day	National Biology Olympiad Past papers 2011-2012	National Biology Olympiad Past papers 2013-2014	National Biology Olympiad Past papers 2014-2015	National Biology Olympiad Past papers 2016 - Present
WEEK 2	2. The Chemical Context of Life 3. Water and Life Khan Academy: Chemistry of life, Acids, bases	4. Carbon and the Molecular Diversity of Life 5. The Structure and Function of Large Biological Molecules	Rest day	Khan Academy: Properties of carbon 6. A Tour of the Cell Khan Academy: Structure of a cell	7. Membrane Structure and Function Khan Academy: Membranes and transport	8. An Introduction to Metabolism 9. Cellular Respiration and Fermentation Khan Academy: Energy; Enzymes;	10. Photosynthesis 12. The Cell Cycle Khan Academy: Cellular respiration Photosynthesis; Cell division
WEEK 3	11. Cell Communica-tion Khan Academy: Cell signaling	13. Meiosis and Sexual Life Cycles	Rest day	14. Mendel and the Gene Idea	15. The Chromosomal Basis of Inheritance	16. The Molecular Basis of Inheritance	Khan Academy: Classical and molecular genetics; DNA as the genetic material
WEEK 4	17. From Gene to Protein Khan Academy: Central dogma	18. Regulation of Gene Expression Khan Academy: Gene regulation	Rest day	19. Viruses Khan Academy: Viruses	20. Biotechnology Khan Academy: Biotechnology; Developmental biology	21. Genomes and Their Evolution Khan Academy: Evolution and the tree of life	22. Descent with Modification: A Darwinian View of Life 23. The Evolution of Populations 24. The Origin of Species

WEEK 5	25. The History of Life on Earth Khan academy: History of life on Earth	26. Phylogeny and the Tree of Life	Rest day	27. Bacteria and Archaea Khan academy: Bacteria and archaea	28. Protists	29. Plant Diversity I: How Plants Colonized Land 30. Plant Diversity II: The Evolution of Seed Plants 31. Fungi	35. Plant Structure, Growth, and Development 36. Resource Acquisition and Transport in Vascular Plants Khan Academy: Plant biology
WEEK 6	37. Soil and Plant Nutrition	38. Angiosperm Reproduction	Rest day	39. Plant Responses to Internal and External Signals	32. Overview of Animal Diversity	33. Introduction to Invertebrates 34. The Origin and Evolution of Vertebrates	40. Basic Principles of Animal Form and Function 41. Animal Nutrition Khan academy: Principles of Physiology
WEEK 7	42. Circulation and Gas Exchange	43. The Immune System Khan academy: Human biology	Rest day	44. Osmoregulation and Excretion Khan academy: Human biology	45. Hormones and the Endocrine System	46. Animal Reproduction Khan academy: Developmental biology	Khan academy: Human biology
WEEK 8	47. Animal Development	48. Neurons, Synapses, and Signaling	Rest day	49. Nervous Systems	50. Sensory and Motor Mechanisms	51. Animal Behavior 52. An Introduction to Ecology Khan academy: Behavioral biology	53. Population Ecology 54. Community Ecology Khan academy: Biodiversity and conservation

WEEK 9	55. Ecosystems and Restoration Ecology	Genetics Extensions of Mendelian Inheritance	Rest day	Genetics Linkage and Genetic Mapping in Eukaryotes	Genetics Genetic Transfer and Mapping in Bacteria and Bacteriophages	Genetics Non-Mendelian Inheritance Variation in Chromosome Structure and Number	Genetics Molecular Structure of DNA and RNA, Chromosome Organization and Molecular Structure, DNA Replication
WEEK 10	Genetics Gene Transcription and RNA Modification	Genetics Translation of mRNA	Rest day	Genetics Gene Regulation in Bacteria and Bacteriophages	Genetics Gene Regulation in Eukaryotes	Genetics Recombinant DNA Technology Biotechnology	Genetics Analysis of DNA Population Genetics Evolutionary Genetics
WEEK 11	Biochemistry Amino Acids Structure of Proteins	Biochemistry Globular Proteins	Rest day	Biochemistry Fibrous Proteins	Biochemistry Enzymes	Biochemistry Bioenergetics and Oxidative Phosphorylation, Glycolysis, Tricarboxylic Acid Cycle	Biochemistry Introduction to Carbohydrates, Gluconeogenesis, Glycogen Metabolism
WEEK 12	Biochemistry Metabolism of Carbohydrates	Biochemistry Pentose Phosphate Pathway and NADPH	Rest day	Biochemistry Metabolism of Dietary Lipids	Biochemistry Fatty Acid and Triacylglycerol Metabolism	Biochemistry Amino Acids, Disposal of Nitrogen, Insulin and Glucagon	Biochemistry Nutrition, Vitamins Biotechnology and Human Disease
WEEK 13	Human Physiology Principles of Neural and Hormonal Communication	Human Physiology Muscle Physiology	Rest day	Human Physiology Body Defenses	Human Physiology The Respiratory System	Human Physiology Cardiac Physiology The Blood Vessels and Blood Pressure The Blood	Human Physiology The Urinary System Fluid and Acid–Base Balance
WEEK 14	Human Physiology The Digestive System	Human Physiology Energy Balance and Temperature Regulation	Rest day	Human Physiology Principles of Endocrinology The Peripheral Endocrine Glands	Human Physiology The Reproductive System	Plant Biology The Molecular Composition of Plant Cells The Plant Cell and Cell Cycle	Plant Biology The Movement of Substances into and out of Cells Respiration Photosynthesis

WEEK 15	Plant Biology Plant Biotechnology	Plant Biology The Process of Evolution	Rest day	Plant Biology Plant systematics	Plant Biology Prokaryotes and Viruses	Plant Biology Fungi Protists: Algae and Heterotrophic Protists	Plant Biology Bryophytes Seedless Vascular Plants Gymnosperms
WEEK 16	Plant Biology Introduction to the Angiosperms Evolution of the Angiosperms	Plant Biology Early Development of the Plant Body	Rest day	Plant Biology Cells and Tissues of the Plant Body	Plant Biology The Root: Structure and Development	Plant Biology The Shoot Plant Hormones	Plant Biology External Factors and Plant Growth Plant Nutrition and Soils The Movement of Water and Solutes
WEEK 17	Molecular Biology of the Cell	Molecular Biology of the Cell Proteins	Rest day	Molecular Biology of DNA, Chromosomes and Genomes	Molecular Biology of the Cell How Cells Read the Genome: From DNA to Protein	Molecular Biology of the Cell Control of Gene Expression Manipulating Proteins, DNA and RNA	Molecular Biology of the Cell Membrane Structure, Membrane Transport, Electrical Properties of Membranes
WEEK 18	Molecular Biology of the Cell Energy Conversion in Mitochondria and Chloroplasts	Molecular Biology of the Cell Sexual Reproduction	Rest day	Molecular Biology of the Cell Pathogens, Infection, and Innate Immunity	Molecular Biology of the Cell The Adaptive Immune System	MIT Course 5.07SC (Fall 2013) - Module I	MIT Course 5.07SC (Fall 2013) - Module II
WEEK 19	MIT Course 5.07SC (Fall 2013) - Module III	MIT Course 7.03 (Fall 2004)	Rest day	MIT Course 7.03 (Fall 2004)	MIT Course 7.03 (Fall 2004)	MIT Course 7.03 (Fall 2004)	MIT Course 7.03 (Fall 2004)
WEEK 20	MIT Course 7.06 (Spring 2007)	MIT Course 7.06 (Spring 2007)	Rest day	MIT Course 7.06 (Spring 2007)	MIT Course 7.06 (Spring 2007)	MIT Course 7.01SC (Fall 2011)	MIT Course 7.01SC (Fall 2011)
WEEK 21	MIT Course 7.01SC (Fall 2011)	MIT Course 7.01SC (Fall 2011)	Rest day	MIT Course 7.012 (Fall 2004)	MIT Course 7.012 (Fall 2004)	MIT Course 7.012 (Fall 2004)	MIT Course 7.012 (Fall 2004)

WEEK 22	MIT Course 7.012 (Fall 2004)	MIT Course 7.013 (Spring 2006)	Rest day	MIT Course 7.013 (Spring 2006)	MIT Course 7.013 (Spring 2006)	MIT Course 7.013 (Spring 2006)	MIT Course 7.013 (Spring 2013)
WEEK 23	MIT Course 7.013 (Spring 2013)	MIT Course 7.013 (Spring 2013)	Rest day	MIT Course 7.013 (Spring 2013)	MIT Course 7.014 (Spring 2005)	MIT Course 7.014 (Spring 2005)	MIT Course 7.014 (Spring 2005)
WEEK 24	MIT Course 7.014 (Spring 2005)	MIT Course 7.014 (Spring 2005)	Rest day	MIT Course 7.016 (Fall 2014)	MIT Course 7.016 (Fall 2014)	MIT Course 7.016 (Fall 2014)	MIT Course 7.016 (Fall 2014)
WEEK 25	IBO Past papers 2004-2005	IBO Past papers 2006-2007	IBO Past papers 2008-2009	IBO Past papers 2010-2011	IBO Past papers 2012-2013	IBO Past papers 2014-2015	IBO Past papers 2016-Present
WEEK 26	MCAT Biological and Biochemical Foundations of Living Systems Practice problems	MCAT Biological and Biochemical Foundations of Living Systems Practice problems	Rest day	MCAT Biological and Biochemical Foundations of Living Systems Practice problems	MCAT Biological and Biochemical Foundations of Living Systems Practice problems	MCAT Biological and Biochemical Foundations of Living Systems Practice problems	MCAT Biological and Biochemical Foundations of Living Systems Practice problems

19 MUST KNOW BIOLOGY TOPICS

> **"Nobody cares how much you know,
> until they know how much you care."**
> *Theodore Roosevelt*

Biology is evolving at an unprecedented rate and you've got to keep up with this pace if you want to be successful. I can't help overemphasizing the importance of finding the right balance between knowledge and reasoning skills. In the previous chapters, we talked about how to develop critical thinking and problem solving skills. Here, we'll focus more on what knowledge you need to have. Some topics are more common in the olympiad than others and this means that you need to allocate enough time to learn them. Molecular biology, Cell biology, and Biochemistry are by far the hardest but also the most common topics in the olympiad, and so below you'll find a list of the must know topics from these fields for the olympiad. You'll also find a list of topics for Plant Biology, Genetics, Human Biology, and Zoology.

Cell biology

Compartmentalization of eukaryotic cells. Structure and function of the cell membrane, the endomembrane system, and organelles. Comparison between eukaryotic and prokaryotic cells.

Intracellular movement of organelles. Cytoskeleton (actin microfilaments, microtubules, intermediate filaments). Mechanism of vesicular transport. Coat proteins, SNAREs, clathrin. Mechanism of cell motility (pseudopodia, cilia, flagella).

Membrane Transport. Active and passive transport. Transport proteins (channels and carriers). Bulk transport (exocytosis and endocytosis). Intracellular sorting.

Cell cycle. The role of cyclins and cyclin dependent protein kinases. Checkpoints. Regulation of G0/G1, G1/S and G2/M.

Extracellular matrix. Cell communication. Cell-cell junctions: tight junctions, gap junctions, adherens junctions, and desmosomes. Cell-matrix junctions: focal adhesions and hemidesmosomes. Plasmodesmata.

Electrical Signaling. Action potentials. EPSP and IPSP. Nernst equation. Neurotransmitters. Voltage-gated channels.

Intracellular signaling. Secondary messenger systems (including Ca^{2+}, IP_3, DAG, cAMP, protein kinases, calmodulin). Cell receptors (GPCRs, RTKs, ligand-gated channels).

Cell division (binary fission, mitosis and meiosis). Cytokinesis in plants and animals. Cancer formation and transformation of the cells.

Apoptosis. Extrinsic and intrinsic mechanisms. The role of caspases, phosphatidylserine, and mitochondria.

Biochemistry

Lugol solution. Benedict's solution. Biuret reaction. Fehling reaction. Tollen's reagent. Sudan solution. Ninhydrin solution. Bradford reagent.

Calculations with chemical formulas and equations. Mass and moles of substance. Molar concentrations. Dilutions and a dilution factor. Serial dilutions. Acids and Bases. Molecular weight, molar mass, Avogadro's number, mass percentage, molar concentration.

Acid base theories: The Arrhenius concept, Lewis concept, Bronsted-Lowry concept. The pH and pOH of a solution. The pH scale. Definition of pKa and pKb. Conjugated acids and bases. The Henderson-Hasselbalch equation. Buffers. Physiological buffers (hemoglobin, phosphate and carbonic acid/hydrogen carbonate buffer). Respiratory and metabolic acidosis and alkalosis. Titration.

Partial pressure. Decompression sickness. Effects of temperature and pressure on solubility of solids and gases. Henry's law.

Amino acid classification: aliphatic and aromatic side chains, branched chain amino acids, sulfur-containing amino acids, acidic and basic amino acids. Methods of protein purification and determination of protein concentrations.

Isoelectric point. Isoelectric focusing.

Definition of primary, secondary, tertiary, and quaternary structure, types of bonds and interactions at each level. Fibrous proteins: α-keratin, silk fibroin, actin, and collagen. Globular proteins: myoglobin, hemoglobin.

Oxygen dissociation curves for myoglobin and hemoglobin. Function of CO_2, BPG, and pH. The Bohr-effect and Haldane effect. R and T forms of hemoglobin.

Definition of enzyme activity, specific enzyme activity, and turnover number. Enzyme effects on the equilibrium constant and on the activation energy. The lock-and-key and induced fit model. Proteolytic activation of zymogens. First, second, third, and zero orders. Half-life of chemical reactions.

The Michaelis-Menten enzyme kinetics. The Michaelis constant. Maximal velocity. Graphic evaluation of V_{max} and K_M using Lineweaver-Burk plot. Isoenzymes. Zymogens. Apoenzymes. Holoenzymes. Cofactors.

Reversible inhibition of enzymes. Competitive, uncompetitive, and non-competitive inhibition. Mixed inhibition. Control of enzyme activity by allosteric regulation. Sigmoidal curves.

Post-translational modification of proteins (e.g. phosphorylation, acetylation, glycosylation). Protein kinases and phosphatases.

Carbohydrate classification, structure and function. Monosaccharides: Aldoses (glyceraldehyde, ribose, deoxyribose, glucose, galactose) and ketoses (dihydroxyacetone, ribulose, fructose). Structure and classification of disaccharides (reducing and non-reducing disaccharides). Structure and function of polysaccharides (glycogen, starch, cellulose, and chitin). Glycosaminoglycans.

Lipid classification. Triglyceride structure. Fatty acid nomenclature, function, classification. Phospholipid structure, function, and classification (including phosphatidylserine, phosphatidylcholine, and phosphatidylinositol). Sphingolipids. Glycolipids. Structure and function of cholesterol, steroid hormones, and lipid soluble vitamins. Arachidonic acid and eicosanoid function.

Absorption of lipids in the small intestine. Metabolism of chylomicrons. Mobilization of fatty acids in adipose tissue, its regulation, and transport in circulation.

Beta oxidation of fatty acids in peroxisomes and mitochondria. Synthesis of fatty acids in the cytoplasm and smooth ER.

Ketogenesis, ketosis, ketone bodies (acetone, beta-hydroxybutyrate, and acetoacetate).

Ribonucleotides and deoxyribonucleotides. Three dimensional structure of DNA (including A, Z, and B forms). Three dimensional structure of RNAs. Structure and function of nucleotides. Coenzyme A, NAD(P), and FAD.

Spectrophotometry. Determination of the absorption spectrum. Beer-Lambert law.

Cellular respiration. ATP structure and its function in coupled reactions. Localization, regulation, function, and enzymes of:

1.   Glycolysis
2.   Pyruvate oxidation (Pyruvate Dehydrogenase complex)
3.   The tricarboxylic acid cycle
4.   The electron transport chain: components, function, and inhibitors.

Mechanism of oxidative phosphorylation. The chemiosmotic hypothesis. Mitochondrial ATPase (Fo F1-ATP-ase). Mitochondrial transport of reducing equivalents (shuttle systems).

Respiratory control, respiratory quotient, P/O ratio, uncoupling of oxidative phosphorylation. Glucose phosphorylation and its role. Glyoxylate cycle.

Comparison of energetics, location, and enzymes of aerobic and anaerobic glucose breakdown (lactic acid fermentation and ethanol fermentation).

Carbohydrate absorption in the intestines. The role, localization, and function of GLUT family glucose transporters. Gluconeogenesis. Hormonal and allosteric regulation of gluconeogenesis in the liver.

The oxidative and non-oxidative branches of pentose-phosphate pathway and their roles.

Reactions of the urea cycle and its regulation. The transport of ammonia, the role of glutamine and alanine (the glutamine cycle).

The thermodynamics of biochemical pathways. Reversible and irreversible reactions. Spontaneous reactions. The central role of ATP in the energetics of cells. Reducing equivalents. The first and second laws of thermodynamics. Enthalpy and entropy. Gibbs free enthalpy change.

Cori cycle and glucose-alanine cycle: enzymes, location, regulation, and function.

Glycogenesis. Glycogenolysis. Mobilization of glycogen in liver and muscle.

Photosynthesis. Pigments. Light-dependent reactions and light-independent reactions: enzymes, location, and role. C3, C4, and CAM plants.

Molecular biology

The properties and functions of DNA polymerases I, II, and III. Reverse transcription in retroviruses.

The reactions catalyzed by DNA ligase, primase, helicase, gyrase, topoisomerases, exonucleases, and endonucleases.

The initiation of DNA replication in prokaryotes and eukaryotes. Okazaki fragments and leading strands.

The organization of the prokaryotic genome and eukaryotic genome (condensation levels, structure of nucleosomes, euchromatin, heterochromatin). Monocistronic and polycistronic DNA.

The most frequent mutations of DNA. Repair mechanisms. Point mutations (substitutions (transitions, transversions), frameshift mutations, suppressor mutations).

Mechanism of transcription. Differences and similarities between transcription in prokaryotes and eukaryotes. The properties and functions of RNA polymerase I, II, and III. The eukaryotic promoters and the role of enhancers and silencers. The structure of monocistronic mRNA. The TATA box.

The structure and role of the promoters in prokaryotes. The elongation and termination of transcription in prokaryotes (rho-dependent and rho-independent mechanisms). The structure of polycistronic mRNA. The Pribnow box.

Post-transcriptional modifications of the eukaryotic primary transcript at the 5' end and at the 3' end. Splicing. The mechanism of alternative splicing.

Gene expression regulation in prokaryotes. The structure of inducible and repressible operons. Positive and negative regulation of the operons. Examples of *lac* and *trp* operon (including attenuation).

Gene expression regulation in eukaryotes. Transcriptional, post-transcriptional, and translational control. mRNA lifespan and degradation. Translational control in eukaryotes.

Mechanism of translation. Differences and similarities of translation in prokaryotes and eukaryotes. Shine-Dalgarno sequence. The termination of translation in prokaryotes and eukaryotes.

The structure and function of tRNA molecules. The formation of aminoacyl-tRNAs.

The structure, function, and assembly of ribosomal subunits into ribosomes.

The role and characteristics of signal sequences at C-terminus or N-terminus and of signal recognition particles. Nuclear import and export. Transport of proteins to different organelles. Coat proteins, SNAREs, and exocytosis of proteins.

Lysosomes and ubiquitin-proteasome pathway. Receptor-mediated endocytosis. Disposal of proteins. Heat-shock proteins and chaperones.

Tumorigenesis and malignant transformation of cells. The role of proto-oncogenes, oncogenes, and tumor suppressor genes.

Molecular biology techniques (gene cloning, polymerase chain reaction, gel electrophoresis, gel retardation assay, chromatin immunoprecipitation assay, expression vectors, reporter genes (e.g. GFP, luciferase), genomic and cDNA libraries, colony hybridization, Southern, Northern, and Western blotting, DNA chip technology, genetic and physical maps, karyotyping, dideoxynucleotide chain termination reaction and other DNA sequencing method, DNA fingerprinting, hybridization, replica plating, RFLP, Ames test, etc.).

Must know topics for Plant Biology, Genetics, Human Anatomy & Physiology, and Zoology are outlined below. Make sure you have an in-depth understanding of each topic as these form the core of the biology olympiad.

Plant biology

The Molecular Composition of Plant Cells, The Plant Cell Organelles, Cells and Tissues of the Plant Body, Cellular Movement of Substances, Photosynthesis, Fungi, Algae and Protists, Bryophytes, Seedless Vascular Plants, Gymnosperms, Angiosperms, Structure and Development of The Roots, Structure and Development of The Shoots Secondary Growth, Plant Hormones, External Factors and Plant Growth, Plant Nutrition, The Movement of Water and Solutes in Plants.

Genetics

Mendelian Inheritance, Extensions of Mendelian Inheritance, Linkage and Genetic Mapping in Eukaryotes, Genetic Transfer and Mapping in Bacteria and Bacteriophages, Non-Mendelian Inheritance, Variation in Chromosome Structure and Number, Molecular Structure of DNA and RNA, Chromosome Organization and Structure, DNA Replication, Transcription and RNA Modification, Translation, Gene Regulation in Bacteria, Gene Regulation in Eukaryotes, Gene Mutation and DNA Repair, Biotechnology.

Human physiology & anatomy

Principles of Neurocrine, Autocrine, Paracrine, and Endocrine Communication, The Central Nervous System, The Peripheral Nervous System, Special Senses, The Endocrine System, The Musculoskeletal System, The Respiratory System, The Cardiovascular System (Heart, Blood Vessels, and Blood), The Immune System, The Urinary System, Fluid and Acid-Base Balance, The Digestive System, Energy Balance and Temperature Regulation, The Reproductive System, Embryonic Development

Zoology

Classification of Animals, Phylogeny of Animals, Protozoans, Radiate Animals (Cnidaria, Ctenophora), Acoelomate Animals (Platyhelminthes, Nemertea), Pseudocoelomate Animals (Rotifers, Nematodes), Mollusca (Gastropoda, Bivalvia, Cephalopoda), Segmented Worms (Annelida, Hirudinea, Polychaeta), Arthropods (Insecta, Arachnida, Crustacea), Aquatic and Terrestrial Mandibulates, Protostomes, Deuterostomes (Echinoderms, Hemichordates, Chordates), Fish, Amphibians, Reptiles, Birds, Mammals (Eutherians, Marsupials, Monotremes), Animal Ecology.

20 CHEMISTRY AND PHYSICS IN THE BIOLOGY OLYMPIAD

> **"You cannot teach a man anything;**
> **you can only help him discover it in himself."**
> *Galileo*

Students usually ask me about the importance of chemistry and physics for the biology olympiads. Unfortunately, there is no straightforward answer but I can assure you that knowing the basics of chemistry and physics will help you immensely. I'm not talking about reaching the level of the IChO or IPhO but a high school-level understanding of physical and chemical laws will be a great asset in any biology olympiad. Let me give you some examples where chemistry and physics really help. Head to the IBO website and look for the IBO 2014 Theoretical Test Part A Question 12, which talks about Poiseuille's Law. Or the USABO Open Exam 2016 Question 5, which talks about resistance and conductance. Question 9 in that same paper and Question 5 in the IBO 2012 Singapore Theoretical Test Paper 1 are both nice examples of questions where an understanding of chemistry, pH and pKa values comes in handy.

For chemistry, you should be familiar with the following concepts:

- Molecular interactions (including different types of bonds)
- Metal ions and metal complexes
- Structure and polarity of liquid water
- Ionic compounds in aqueous solutions
- Acid-base equilibria, pH, pKa and pKb values, indicators, the Henderson-Hasselbalch equation
- Hydrophobic effect
- Stoichiometry of chemical reactions
- Functional groups and their properties
- Enthalpy, entropy, and Gibbs free energy

- Equilibrium constant
- Temperature dependence of equilibria
- Electrochemistry, electrochemical cells, Nernst equation
- Reaction rate laws and kinetic order
- Transition states
- Temperature dependence of kinetics
- Catalysis, enzyme-catalyzed reactions, and the Michaelis-Menten equation
- Chemical structures of biomolecules: proteins, nucleic acids, lipids, and polysaccharides
- Molecular assemblies: micelles, liposomes, monolayers, biological membranes

For physics, you don't need to know any formulas by heart as you won't be asked to calculate anything but you should be confident with the following topics:

- Forces and Newton's laws of motion
- Work and energy
- Fluids (liquids, laminar flow, viscosity, turbulence)
- Thermodynamics
- Electric charge, field, and potential
- Light and the electromagnetic spectrum (waves, light, optics, and imaging)
- Radioactivity and half lives

There are some physics laws that are worth reviewing for the olympiad. Read about Ohm's law, Poiseuille's law, Dalton's Law, Boyle's law, Charles' law, Laplace's Law, Gibbs free energy equation, ideal gas law, rate laws and equilibria, phase solubility rules, and laws of thermodynamics.

Note that you'll never be asked to calculate anything from physics or chemistry unless you are given a specific formula where you just need to plug numbers in. This means that you don't need to know the formulas per se, but you should be able to understand the relationship between each variable. For example, as the diameter of the blood vessel increases, blood pressure decreases (which you can also deduce if you look at the formula of Poiseuille's law).

21 MATH SKILLS IN BIOLOGY OLYMPIADS

> *"The study of mathematics, like the Nile,*
> *begins in minuteness but ends in magnificence."*
> *Charles Caleb Colton*

It goes without saying that mathematics is a crucial and very common subject in any biology olympiad. Remember a Chi square formula or a Student's t-test with standard deviations? Or finding probabilities from a Punnett square? Or the Beer-Lambert law and standard curves? All of these types of questions require a sound understanding of core mathematical concepts. It's a no-brainer that having a range of mathematical skills will enable you to score better in the biology olympiad. I've outlined the essential math topics that you need to know for the olympiad in **Table 10.**

Table 10 Key Math Topics In Biology Olympiads

Arithmetic calculations	Convert between units, know unit prefixes, do calculations, use fractions, standard forms, decimals, significant figures, round numbers, use ratios, fractions, percentages, work with power, exponential, logarithmic functions, know index notation and reciprocals, and work with proportionality.
Algebra	Solve algebraic equations, use logarithms, and work with equations.
Graphs	Interpret and analyze data from tables and graphs, including charts, line graphs, scatter graphs, bar charts, pie charts, and stacked bar charts, understand independent variables and dependent variables, gradients, slopes, time series, determine intercepts of the graph, understand random error, quartile, box plot, and outliers, ranges, and scales.

Geometry and trigonometry	Calculate the surface area, volume, and circumference of common shapes that are relevant to biology.
Probabilities and statistics	Work with probabilities, independent events, combined events, risk, probability distributions, correlation, and independence, the chi-squared test to test the significance of the difference between observed and expected results, the Student's t-test to compare the difference between two means, the correlation coefficient, e.g., Spearman's Rank Correlation Coefficient to look for an association between two sets of data, calculate means, modes, medians, standard deviations, p-values, two-tailed and one-tailed test, null and alternative hypotheses.

Also, I've compiled a list of useful formulas that you should know for the olympiad (**Table 11**).

Table 11 Biology Olympiad Formula Sheet

Hardy-Weinberg Equilibrium (for two alleles)	$p^2 + 2pq + q^2 = 1$ $p + q = 1$ p = frequency of the dominant allele in the population q = frequency of the recessive allele in the population p^2 = frequency of homozygous dominant individuals q^2 = frequency of homozygous recessive individuals $2pq$ = frequency of heterozygous individuals
Hardy-Weinberg Equilibrium (for three alleles)	$p + q + r = 1$ $p^2 + 2pq + 2pr + 2rq + q^2 + r^2 = 1$
Bacterial growth	$N(t) = N_0 2^{t/d}$ N_0 = the number of cells in generation 0, t = total time taken for divisions, d = doubling time
Beer-Lambert Law	$A = \log_{10} \frac{I_0}{I} = \varepsilon l c$
Standard deviation	$\sigma = \sqrt{\dfrac{\Sigma (X - \underline{X})^2}{n-1}}$

Standard error

$$SE_{\bar{x}} = \frac{s_x}{\sqrt{n}}$$

Variance

$$S^2 = \frac{\Sigma(X-\bar{X})^2}{N-1}$$

Student's t-test

$$t = \frac{\bar{x}_1 - \bar{x}_2}{\sqrt{\frac{s_1^2}{N_1} + \frac{s_2^2}{N_2}}}$$

Chi-Square

$$X^2 = \Sigma\,\frac{(o-e)^2}{e}$$

Magnification   Magnification = size of image / size of actual object

Circumference of circle $2\pi r$

Area of circle πr^2

Volume of cuboid   hbl

Mean

$$\bar{x} = \frac{\Sigma x}{n}$$

% yield

$$\frac{actual\ amount}{theoretical\ amount} \times 100$$

Percentage change

$$\frac{new\ quantity - original\ quantity}{original\ quantity} \times 100$$

Retardation factor (chromatography)

$$Rf = \frac{distance\ moved\ by\ the\ solute}{distance\ moved\ by\ the\ solvent}$$

pH and pOH

pH = -log[H_3O^+]
pOH = -log[OH^-]
pH + pOH = 14

Henderson-Hasselbalch equation

$$pH = pK_a + \log_{10}\left(\frac{[A^-]}{[HA]}\right)$$

pKa	$pK_a = log_{10}(K_a)$
The free energy of a reaction	$\Delta G = \Delta G^o + RT \ln K_{eq}$
	R is the ideal gas constant in units of J/mol-K, T is the temperature in Kelvin, ln represents a logarithm to the base e, and K is the reaction equilibrium constant.
The standard-state free energy of reaction	$\Delta G_o = - RT \ln K_{eq}$
Gibbs free energy	$\Delta G = \Delta H - T\Delta S$
Doubling time	$t\tfrac{1}{2} = \dfrac{\ln 2}{k} = \dfrac{0.693}{k}$
Charles' Law	$\dfrac{V}{T} = k$ $\dfrac{V_1}{T_1} = \dfrac{V_2}{T_2}$
Boyle's Law	$PV = k$ $P_1 V_1 = P_2 V_2$
Law of mass action	$aA + bB \rightleftharpoons cC + dD$ $K_c = \dfrac{[C]^c [B]^b}{[A]^a [B]^b}$
Poiseuille's law	$Q = \dfrac{\pi P r^4}{8\eta l}$
Dilution factor (DF)	$DF = \dfrac{C_1}{C_2} = \dfrac{V_2}{V_1}$ $C_1 V_1 = C_2 V_2$
	C_1 = original (initial) concentration of the solution, before it gets watered down or diluted C_2 = final concentration of the solution, after dilution V_1 = (initial) volume before dilution V_2 = final volume after dilution

Molarity	$$\frac{\text{\# of mol of solute}}{\text{liter of solution}}$$
Molality	$$\frac{\text{\# of mol of solute}}{\text{kg of solvent}}$$
Michaelis-Menten Kinetics	$$V = \frac{v_{max}[S]}{K_m + [S]}$$
Isoelectric point	$$pI = \frac{pK_{a1} + pK_{a2}}{2}$$
Nernst equation	$$E_{ion} = \frac{61}{z} \log \frac{[ion]_{out}}{[ion]_{in}}$$

Cardiac output (CO)
CO = HR x SV
HR = heart rate, SV = stroke volume

Pulmonary ventilation rate (PVR)
PVR = TV x BR
TV = tidal volume, BR = breathing rate

Lincoln index

$$N = \frac{S_1 \times S_2}{R}$$

S1 = total captured and marked, S2 = total number recaptured
R = number of marked animals recaptures

Net primary production
NPP = GPP - R
R - energy lost in respiration, GPP - gross primary production

Change in population size
dN/dt = B - D
B = birth rate, D = death rate

Growth rate (r)

$$\frac{\Delta N}{\Delta t} = \frac{\text{change in population size}}{\text{change in time}}$$

Logistic growth

$$\frac{\Delta N}{\Delta t} = r_{max} \, N \, \frac{K-N}{K}$$

Exponential growth

$$\frac{\Delta N}{\Delta t} = r_{max} N$$

Respiratory quotient

$$RQ = \frac{CO_2 \; produced}{O_2 \; consumed}$$

Water Potential (Ψ)

$\Psi = \Psi_P + \Psi_S$
Ψ_P = pressure potential Ψ_S = solute potential

Key power laws

$x^n * x^m = x^{n+m}$ multiplicative rule

$\frac{x^n}{x^m} = x^{n-m}$ division rule

$(x^n)^m = x^{nm}$ power rule

$x^{-1} = \frac{1}{x^n}$ reciprocal rule

$x^{n/m} = \sqrt[m]{x^n}$ root rule

Binomial distribution

$$\frac{n!}{x!(n-x)!} \; p^x q^{n-x}$$

The number of gene pairs

Number of gene pairs	Number of phenotypes	Number of genotypes	Proportion of homozygotes for all genes
1	2	3	1/2
2	4	9	1/4
3	8	27	1/8
4	16	81	1/16
n	2^n	3^n	$(\frac{1}{2})^n$

Total number of genotypes

$2^{(2 * \text{number of hybrid genes})}$

For example, for monohybrid crosses, Total = $2^{(2*1)} = 4$; for dihybrid, Total = $2^{(2*2)} = 16$; for trihybrid, Total = $2^{(2*3)} = 64$

Determining the Number of Categories of Phenotypes

$(2n + 1)$, where n = the number of gene pairs

Determining the Number of Genes

$1/4^n = P$, where P = proportion of F2 individuals expressing either of the two most extreme phenotypes, n = the number of gene pairs

Coefficient of relatedness	$1/2^n$, where n^{th} level ancestor of descendant

Fitness

$$p^2 w_{11} + 2pqw_{12} + q^2 w_{22} = \overline{w}$$

$$p^2 \frac{w_{11}}{\overline{w}} + 2pq \frac{w_{12}}{\overline{w}} + q^2 \frac{w_{22}}{\overline{w}} = 1.0$$

Degrees of freedom

Df = n–1, where n = total number of categories

Df = (r-1)(c-1), where **r** represents the number of **rows** in the two-way table and **c** represents the number of **columns**.

Recombination frequency

$$RF = \frac{\# \ of \ recombinants}{\# \ total \ offspring} \times 100\%$$

Combination formula

$\frac{n!}{(n-r)! \ r!}$, use combination when the order does not matter.

Permutation formula

$\frac{n!}{(n-r)!}$, use permutation when the order does matter.

Concentration of the solution

$V \times c = n$
V = volume (L), c = molarity (M), n = number of moles (mol)

Logarithms

$\log_a x = k$, $a^k = x$

Shannon index of diversity

$$H = -\Sigma \ pi \ ln \ pi \ ,$$
where p_i is the proportion of individuals belonging to the ith species in the population dataset.

Also, don't forget the key prefixes, which will save your life in practicals:

Factor	Prefix	Symbol
10^9	giga	G
10^6	mega	M
10^3	kilo	k
10^{-2}	centi	c
10^{-3}	milli	m
10^{-6}	micro	μ
10^{-9}	nano	n
10^{-12}	pico	p

22 DEVELOPING PRACTICAL SKILLS

> *"Success is a ladder you cannot climb
> with your hands in your pockets."*
> *American Proverb*

I know that developing lab skills is the hardest part of the biology olympiad. You might have to extract DNA from a cell sample and run a gel electrophoresis, prepare slides of plant cells, or identify unknown invertebrate species using a taxonomy book. We are rarely taught how to do such experiments step-by-step in school. Usually, you just get some instructions and are left alone to develop your practical skills by trial and error. In fact, mainly because of lack of experience in the lab I screwed up both of my IBOs (see section 'My Experience In Biology Olympiads'). Painful as it is, you need to perfect those skills. So let me share a list of techniques that are important for the biology olympiad. Note that it's non-exhaustive but should serve as a good reference point. Ready?

Cell biology

Use of a Microtome to Make Slides, Centrifugation, Cell Fractionation, Different Types of Microscopy, Immunostaining, Histology, Haemocytometer, Drawing of Preparations, Maceration and Squash Technique, Smear Method, Staining of Cells.

Biochemistry

Acid-base Equilibrium, K_{eq} Values, Spectrophotometry (Beer-Lambert Law), Net Charges of Amino Acids and Peptides, Titration Curves of Amino Acids, Chromatography (Affinity, Ion-exchange, Size-exclusion, Paper Chromatography And Rf Values), Colorimetry, Enzyme Kinetics, Calculating Rate of Enzyme Reaction, Enzyme Inhibition (Lineweaver-Burk Plot, Michaelis-Menten Equation), DNA Extraction, Serial Dilutions, Concentrations,

Molar Solutions, pH and Buffers, Henderson-Hasselbalch Equation, Pipetting Liquids, Protein Purification, Protein Quantification, Microfiltration and Dialysis, Calibration Curves, Testing For Lipids, Proteins and Carbohydrates (Biuret's Test, Sudan Test, Ninhydrin Test, Lugol's Solution Test, Benedict's Solution Test, Fehling Reaction, Tollens' Reagent Test, Bradford Protein Assay, Paper Bag Test).

Molecular biology

2D Electrophoresis, PAGE, Gel Electrophoresis, SDS-PAGE, Isoelectric Focusing, Western Blot, Northern Blot, Southern Blot, Eastern Blot, Hybridization, Immunoprecipitation Assay, ELISA, DNA Fingerprinting, Genetic Engineering, Restriction Endonucleases, Restriction Maps, RFLP, Fish, G-stain, Dideoxy Chain Termination Reaction, Polymerase Chain Reaction (PCR), RT-PCR, RNA Interference, Genetic Manipulation, CRISPR-Cas9 System.

Genetics

Analyzing Pedigree Charts, Creating Punnett Squares, Chi-square of Genetic Data (Goodness Of Fit), Interpreting DNA Profiles, Identifying Recombinants, Dihybrid Cross & Trihybrid Cross, Mapping Genes, Deriving Linkage Distance and Gene Order.

Plant biology

Potometry, Making Sections of Plant Materials, Identifying Plant Structures and Organs (Leaves, Stems, Roots, Flowers, Fruits, etc.), Recognizing Major Plant Groups (e.g. Algae, Mosses, Ferns, and Spermatophytes), Floral Morphology, Floral Formulas and Diagrams, Staining and Slide Preparation of Plant Organs and Tissues, Measurement of Photosynthesis And Transpiration.

Evolution, ethology, phylogenetics, ecology

Identification Keys for Various Organisms, Observation and Interpretation of Animal Behavior (Habituation And Sensitization, Associative Learning (Classical Conditioning and Associative Learning), Social Learning, Foraging Behavior, Imprinting, Insight, Latent Learning), Construction Of Simple Dichotomous Keys, UPGMA, Identification of the Most Common Flowering Plant Families, Identification of Insect Orders, Identification of Phyla and Classes of Organisms, Hardy-Weinberg Formula, Estimation of Population Density and Growth, Biomass, Water and Air Quality, Quadrat Sampling.

Animal biology

Dissections of an Invertebrate (from Annelida, Arthropoda, or Mollusca groups) and Identification of the Main Macroscopic Organs, Whole - Mount Slide Preparation of Small Invertebrates, Elementary Measurement of Respiration.

Microbiology

Bacterial Transformation, Gram Staining, Log Scales, Inoculation and Aseptic Techniques, Bacterial Plating, Bacterial Growth Calculations, Ames test.

Statistics

Chi Square, Student's t-test, Probability and Probability Distributions, Mean, Median, Percentage, Variance, Standard Deviation, Standard Error, Bayes' Theorem, Binomial Expansion Formula.

So, you've got the list - what's next? It's time to find a lab! Ask around at school or at the local university if you could spend some time doing various experiments. Find a supervisor who can guide you through all the practical experience. Work through the above list together with a lab technician or a teacher and make sure you know how to use all of these techniques.

Also, print off past IBO practical exam papers and review them together with your supervisor, teacher, or mentor. You don't necessarily need to carry out the experiments yourself, but instead discuss and plan the strategy and steps you should take to answer the questions. Believe me, understanding how to approach the practical exam will be tremendously useful.

If resources are limited or if you live in the middle of nowhere, that's not a problem at all, mate! Google all of these techniques from the list and look for protocols. Try to understand why each step is needed and what each chemical does. Also, the Internet is full of amazing videos so watch them to get an understanding of what's involved in the experiments, what exactly you need to do, and in what order. Primates are really good at social learning so by observing others doing various experiments, you'll also improve your lab skills.

You say you have no Internet? That's not a problem at all, either! Biology is all around you. Head to the store and buy some whole invertebrates (clams, crabs, snails, shrimp, etc.). Turn your kitchen into the lab! Using your zoology textbook, dissect those tiny animals, identify, and label different parts with pins. Use as many different animals as possible (it's worth checking out the biosystematics list on the IBO website). In the summer, catch some buzzing bugs, butterflies, grasshoppers, crickets, or slimy earthworms in the garden. Dissect them and observe them under a microscope (nowadays, microscopes are dead cheap so either buy one for yourself or borrow one from school). Get some blossoming flowers from grandma's garden, make longitudinal and vertical cross sections of stems, roots, and leaves. Investigate the flower anatomy and try to identify their floral formulas. Learn to draw what you see under the microscope as biological drawings are common in the olympiad, too.

There are practicals in the olympiad that rely merely on theoretical knowledge (e.g., some parts of Plant Biology, Ethology, and Biosystematics) so for these you don't even need the lab. Just read about these topics on the Internet. Also, practice some basic statistics using textbooks and online resources. Usually, the formulas will be provided but understanding what you need to plug into the formulas or what the final numbers mean will be indispensable in the olympiad.

Your success in the practical exam depends not only on knowing different techniques or how to use different tools, but also on measurements and calculations during the experiment. In the olympiad, time is always limited so be sure to:

- Follow written procedures and instructions (highlight and underline if needed, use different colors to highlight the numbering of the steps);

- Understand exactly what is being asked (there's no point in rushing to carry out the experiment if you don't know what the point of it is);

- Accurately take measurements;

- Check if the capacity of the instrument is correct (this is very important when it comes to adjustable volume pipette);

- Don't forget to provide your answers in the proper units (also sometimes you may need to interconvert between micro- and milli- so be attentive!);

- Input the correct numbers in the calculator;

- Work in a neat fashion and show all of your work because you may get extra points;

- Consider whether the answer makes sense;

- Use the last few minutes to check your work and that you've completed all parts.

So now you have the list of techniques that you need to be able to master. But how do you get in the lab? Let's see in the next section.

23 HOW TO GET INTO A LAB

> "Without laboratories men of science
> are soldiers without arms."
> *Louis Pasteur*

Have you ever tried to get a placement in a lab? Were you rejected in 99.9% of cases? I've been there, too. And I know you may feel like banging your head against a wall. Fair enough. Getting experience in a research lab at a university might seem quite (I mean very) daunting. Moreover, if you are under 16, there might be some additional strict limitations as to where you can work and if you can be in the research facilities at all. As you get older, things get easier (don't get me wrong, this applies only to certain things like access to the lab).

Apart from your age, another obstacle is that you, as an intern, will most likely be a tremendous time sink. Just like the nerve cells in your brain, full of GLUT3 glucose transporters, are ravenous sugar sinks (okay I get it, it isn't the best biological analogy, but what can I do, I'm a nerd at heart), you will eat up tons of time being trained and familiarized with the rules in the lab, key techniques, and experiment protocols. Professors, post docs, researchers, and the like are very busy people. Thus, you may find it very difficult to convince them to allow you to conduct a research placement even for a few days. So if you want to give it another shot, I've put together a list of steps that might increase your minuscule chances of getting a placement.

1 Send hundreds of applications to hundreds of people at hundreds of universities

Sound complicated? C'mon, don't get frustrated about this! If you really want to come at least one step closer to success, make sure you send your application to as many institutions and labs as possible. Even try different states or countries.

You see, when I was trying to apply to various research internships as an undergraduate, my success rate was rather gloomy. Out of 80, I got just one in Israel at the Weizmann Institute.

However, things got better later on. In my third year, out of 40 applications, I got four offers. Are you ready to hear the secret? It turned out that the admission officers were actually looking for experience in your personal statement. I don't know how you feel about this, but I was gutted. You're applying for the research intern position to *get* experience but you won't get a place if you don't already *have* experience. Funny, no? The sad thing is that this stupidity exists everywhere. Once, I applied for an internship at an educational charity. I ticked all the boxes in the requirements section but still received the following answer:

"We appreciate the opportunity to consider you for a position on our team. We've reviewed your background and experience and have decided to proceed with other candidates whose skills meet our needs more closely at this time."

So, no matter what skills you want to develop in the internship, you *must* already have them before you apply. Ugh...

So how can you go about this? Try getting *any* experience, no matter how unprestigious or trivial. Just remember that you need to have something to put on your CV to show your keen commitment. Oh, and it goes without saying that you must emphasize your experience in the biology olympiad. This will highlight your academic interest and familiarity with the field.

Note, however, that this tip has two sides. The downside is that if you contact too many people and try to persuade all of them how much you like their research (just imagine you sent an email to close colleagues!), this might appear to them as just fishing in a lake for any opportunity you can get. Why is it bad? Here is the thing - you might seem immature and naive. To avoid this, tailor your requests to each recipient by addressing the letter to the specific person and by mentioning the specific research project you're interested in.

2 Don't be picky

Avoid being picky about the specific research project or lab. Apply anywhere. Everywhere. Chances are, you'll be rejected by many, if not all, of them. I can say that for every 50 emails you send, you will most likely get one or two responses, which will probably say no. Be prepared psychologically and grow a chitin exoskeleton to protect yourself from millions of rejections.

3 Be persistent

As Darwin indicated, there are limited resources for every species, and thus there is constant competition for these resources. In the same way, there are limited spots in the lab, and there is constant competition for research placements. So don't give up when you receive the first few rejections. Keep sending in your applications. Someday, someone will accept you.

Also, don't be offended if you don't hear anything back at all. It's nothing personal. Just imagine there are thousands of teenagers like you trying to get the same position in the same lab with the same supervisor. Scientists can't be bothered to send rejections to everyone. If they don't like your application, they most likely won't even respond.

4 Apply early. Very early

Like, close to 10 months or more in advance. You need to understand that there might be a lot of paperwork and bureaucracy involved in accepting a summer intern (especially a high schooler). So make sure you give your potential supervisor as much time as possible to get ready for your arrival. This will also show that you are thoughtful and able to plan ahead. In contrast, sending requests four weeks in advance shows that you are desperate and selfish.

5 Find research programs for high schoolers

If you apply for a program that welcomes high schoolers, it's much less likely that you'll get rejected. Additionally, you don't have to waste your time emailing ten million people (and trust me, it's annoying and super boring). So dig around like a hungry *Lumbricus terrestris* (nerds...) and see if you can get into one of those programs. If you can't find anything, just keep emailing individual researchers. Prepare for the worst, but hope for the best!

6 Use your networks

Yeah, if you want to get something, use your networks. That's kind of foolproof. Ask your classmates, parents, parents' friends, teachers, and staff at your school if they have any acquaintances at local universities or science labs. Can you really afford not to ask? Trust me, it's much easier to get a place via your connections.

People from the lab will at least know that you are a reliable person and will be assured you don't have any bad intentions. This is actually how I got one of my first experiences in a lab. My best friend had an aunt who worked in a genetics lab. And guess what? The aunt invited my friend, as well as me and my sister to spend a week in the lab doing some cool genetics stuff.

7 Emphasize your intention to work on a voluntary basis

State clearly in your email or official application that you don't expect to get any remuneration and that an extra pair of hands always helps! Emphasizing this will give researchers assurance that you have thought this through and show them that you're truly committed.

8 Ignite the feeling of importance

See things from a scientist's angle. Why on earth would they waste their time with a high schooler? Isn't it better to get a BSc or MSc student instead, who has at least some prior experience in the lab? What would they get in return if they take you instead?

At this point, it's good to start thinking about what you can offer to the scientist. Think hard. One of the things you could do which will benefit both parties is to sign up for a science fair. Check out the Google Science Fair or Intel International Science and Engineering Fair, or any other local competitions. Now you have a legitimate excuse to contact a potential supervisor. In your email, you can offer them the opportunity to support you and get recognition (potentially an award, too). Tell them how popular and competitive the fair or competition is and that supporting you and your project will benefit their institution or lab.

The second option is to search for public engagement awards for scientists. Make a small list. Then, in your application, state that by hosting you in his or her lab, the scientist will be able to apply for that particular prestigious award. Researchers sometimes (or always?) lack the time to stay on top of calls for award nominations as they're already busy with grant applications. If you do some work for them by selecting the specific calls for the award nomination, they'll see that you truly care. And not just about yourself, but most importantly about them.

9 Concentrate on the areas which set you apart from others

Explain in your application why you're better than others. Why are you a better candidate than the university student? Obvious, isn't it? It might be your exceptional programming skills, analytical thinking, ability to learn fast, humor, digital design skills, public speaking skills, excellent computer skills, or maybe impeccable manual dexterity. We all have some exceptional powers hidden somewhere in our flesh.

But you know what? Not everything will do the trick. Think *only* about those skills that will help your supervisor do better research, publish higher quality papers, translate papers to other languages, design nicer posters, analyze data quicker or merely run gel electrophoresis faster. Sell yourself! Who cares if you can bake the best pizza in the world if it won't help your potential supervisor? A rule of thumb is to focus on what you can do for the scientist. If you can highlight such skills and relate them to the scientist's current work, your chances of getting that placement will quadruple. If you can't, don't waste your time and don't apply until you have something to offer to the supervisor.

10 Be succinct

Ask a friend, parent, or teacher to go through your application and CV to edit out any wordy or redundant sentences. Bear in mind, people are busy. When they see something longer than one A4 page, they'll say they don't have time to read all of that. As a result, your CV will be on its way to the bin. So keep your request to one page. And don't be the devil and use a small font to stuff as many things as you can in your application. Also, leave reasonable line spacing to make the application quick and easy to read.

11 Be creative

Scientists receive a ton of applications that look the same. Same font, same boring text, same black and white style. You say it looks professional and neat? No! No! No! You know what? It takes 3 seconds to make a first (and very important) impression. So if all applications are the same, how can you stand out from the crowd? Well, making your application look different will definitely do the trick in less than three seconds. Find some professional, colorful, and artistic templates for CVs and cover letters on the Internet. Surprise the recipient with something courageously elegant and staggeringly different. This will again show that you care. That you invested time to demonstrate that you're different. Creative. Cheerful. In the dull black-and-white science world this might be a like a ray of fluorescence in a failed Western blot. And boom! You're selected.

12 Don't overuse adjectives or superlatives

We all like to boast about anything. Everything. No matter how trivial or colossal it is. No matter whether it's our own or another's achievement. But here's the scary part: the gap between showing off your skills and talents and being arrogant is as small as the diameter of a *Haemophilus influenzae*. How do we avoid this? Simply don't overuse words like '*the best*', '*most famous*', '*prestigious*', etc. Don't write, "You are the best research lab in the city/state/world" or "I am the most hard-working/curious student." Be humble. Otherwise, you risk being accused of being cheap and insincere. Be different. Be realistic. Be *you*.

13 Get some funding

Imagine that in the first paragraph of your email you tell the recipient you've already secured funding. Wanna know a little secret? If you really want to make friends, show that you care about them and that you can solve their problems (this is a great tip from my favorite author, Dale Carnegie who was a developer of famous courses in self-improvement, public speaking, and interpersonal skills). We all think about *ourselves* and how to make *our* lives more enjoyable and less painful. If you can spot the hardships that people around you are trying to conquer, and if you can suggest some potential solutions, you'll never walk alone again. The same applies when you're trying to apply for a research placement. Identify the struggles that scientists face every day and help them overcome them.

You guessed it right - in many cases, it's usually money. Seventy percent of a scientist's time is spent on drafting and crafting grant applications and seeking funding for their research. Now let's imagine that in your application you write "I secured X amount of money for our project this summer". Do you see where I am going with this? Sourcing funds yourself will show that you sincerely believe in what that scientist is doing and that you're ready to donate not only your time, but also money, to the success of the project. This act also shows that you're resourceful, high-flying, and knowledgeable about the climate in science and research.

I know what you're thinking now. Where on earth do I get that money from? Right? There are many options and below you'll find some of them:

1. Google something like 'funding for research placement for school students' or 'financial support for funding voluntary work'.

2. Search for charities and organizations that run and fund placements for high schoolers.

3. Crowdfund and invite all your friends and relatives to donate. It's worth asking and being persistent at this point.

4. Run a marathon and fundraise.

5. Get a temporary job like selling ice-cream or cutting grass for your neighbours (that's what I did when I spent my summer in the USA). Tell people openly and passionately why you need the money. Emphasize that it's your dream to do a research placement and that the work opportunity your 'employers' give to you will immensely help you achieve this. You can also become a freelancer and design posters or leaflets if you have any digital design skills or translate documents if you know any foreign languages.

6. Apply for trusts and foundations as they usually support young people trying to build some professional skills for their future.

7. Enquire about any support from the local council.

8. Contact your school and enquire about any scholarships.

9. Sell stuff that you don't need anymore.

10. Teach students (not only for biology) and help them prepare for school exams.

14 Create your profile on social media

Yes, social media might be your avenue to a research placement. Researchers ranging from PhD students to senior professors have at least a LinkedIn profile so create one for yourself as well. It doesn't matter if you don't have much to put on your profile. I always had the mindset of do-everything-to-enhance-your-CV, and by the end of 12th grade I already had quite a solid résumé (although it was just one page long) full of awards, lab experience, and competitions I took part in.

Use social media to connect with potential supervisors. You see, when you put a face to the name in a world where email is by far the most dominant form of communication, it can be much easier to make a decision about accepting you to the lab. After all, who would like to work with a stranger? Quite unexpectedly, social media somewhat gives assurance that you are a real person. The minute researchers have a face to attach to a name coming into their email inbox, the application you sent will have a whole new tone and meaning. And most likely a positive outcome. So what have you got to lose?

Now that you have learned what you need to do to get a placement, let's have a look at how to design the perfect application letter.

How To Craft A Killer Application Letter

Before you send a ton of emails to your potential supervisors, spend a good amount of time crafting the perfect application letter. First, it's really important to direct it to the person whom you want to work with. Don't you just hate those generic emails which are mass mailed to everyone?

Then, express your eagerness to learn new scientific techniques - this is a must. Indicate if you had a chance to secure funding. Next, show your admiration for that particular researcher and his or her work. You can start somewhere along the lines of "I am fond of your research on x, y, z. In fact, [put in some personal experience around that topic if you have any]. Thus, it would be incredibly interesting for me to work on x, y, z." Most importantly, make it personal. Put some stories from your life to make the application more engaging. Always think that you want to make people think, "Wow, this would be a great student to work with." End the first paragraph by saying why and how this placement will benefit the researcher. No kidding, it's *not* about you, but about the supervisor!

In the second paragraph, highlight your skills and mention at least two to four of your relevant abilities. Please, don't be vague. Exemplify each skill with two to three sentences about your experiences that allowed you to develop or showcase those skills. Don't forget that the application process for the lab internship is like natural selection. Organisms (i.e. you) that have specific traits that are 'fit for purpose' will be selected for survival (i.e. internship). So show your outstanding characteristics and tell the supervisor how your features fit that particular environment (i.e. their lab). Mention all your relevant accomplishments, no matter how minute they are. Be precise. Provide facts, figures, and numbers. After all, this is what scientists love the most - data and stats! Mention your grades, scores in the biology olympiads, and marks you attained in relevant bioscience courses.

In the last paragraph, outline your availability, i.e. hours when you can come and for how long, be it summer or winter break only, part-time, full-time, during the school semester, or throughout the entire school year.

Drafting the perfect email might seem lengthy and burdensome at the beginning, but keep in mind that if you're successful, the experience of participating in the lab project will be invaluable to your future career.

When you've got your cover letter and CV ready, attach them to the email but make your request open ended. What does that mean? Finish the message with some questions. This will show the recipient your level of preparation and interest. It might also enable you to get in contact with other potential supervisors. Craft one or two specific questions that you'd like to learn from the scientist regardless of your request. One question could be, *"Can you recommend any scientists that might be open to high school students like myself for a short research project?"* Or if you want to show your deep interest, ask a question about a specific detail from their research project.

What I would do is find a recently published paper from their lab on the Internet and read the discussion part, where scientists outline future directions and any uncertainties they still have. Take one of the sentences from this section about something that scientists are still unsure about and turn it into a question. For instance, a study by Abedalthagafi *et al.* concluded, *"Now, it is important to critically assess the effect of inhibiting PI3K signaling on tumor progression and response rate in patients with PIK3CA-mutant meningioma in a prospective phase 2 study"* [30]. If you were to email Abedalthagafi's lab, you could ask them, *"To end with, I just wanted to ask about your recent publication on PI3K signaling on tumor progression in the Neuro-Oncology journal. It has been some time since you published that paper and I was just wondering if you finally managed to find any way to inhibit PI3K signaling only in the brain cells but leave other body cells intact?"* It's nothing too fancy but this open question leaves some room for further discussion, possibly even a meeting with a scientist.

So go ahead and prepare your perfect application. Below you'll find an example backbone for a cover letter that you can use.

(Address of the recipient)

Dear Professor/Dr ...,

Paragraph 1: State the name of the institution and briefly explain what attracted you to this particular lab or research project. What can you bring to the lab? How can you help the researchers in their daily work? State why you want to join the lab. Make it personal.

Paragraph 2: Give more details about your educational background (including academic honors, including prizes, awards, etc.), work/voluntary experience, and extracurricular activities. Discuss how your experience relates to the scientist's needs. Tell them **how** you can make their life easier!

Paragraph 3: Describe your interest in what you are applying for. Explain why you are a good candidate (mention special skills like good computer skills, speaking different languages, etc.). Show the reader that you know what their research is about. A killer is to put your own experience that is relevant to that field of research. Mention why getting experience in that lab is important to you personally. Just don't start with, "It will help me get into the best university". It's better to relate it to your personal experience and say something like, "It will help me better understand why my grandpa got Alzheimer's and how I can help him in his daily routine".

Paragraph 4: To end with, add some questions for the recipient to oblige them to reply to you. Also outline your availability including start and end dates. Tell the recipient to contact you if they need further information.

Yours Sincerely,

Your name

Social media accounts (how fancy is that!)

If you got a place - well done! Now you need to prepare for the real battle in the science lab! So get ready because life will get harder when you start your placement. No kidding. See the next section for some tips how to survive in the lab.

24 SURVIVING IN THE LAB

> *"Every failure is a step to success."*
> William Whewell

Almost everyone wants to get a placement in a lab. However, only few know how hard it's to work there. And even fewer are able to deal with all those struggles. I have worked in different labs around the world, including Lithuania, the United Kingdom, Switzerland, and Israel. In the Institute of Medical Sciences in Aberdeen, I experienced cutting edge research on a project asking "Are animals with an extended lifespan due to Nrf2 mediated enhanced antioxidant response less prone to develop Parkinson's disease?". In the NHS Grampian Insulin pump clinic, I was immersed in auditing the insulin pump services. As a participant of Kupcinet-Getz Program, at Weizmann Institute in Israel we investigated how Stat and ERK signalling cooperate to control cellular extensions of escort cells in *Drosophila* ovaries. In Switzerland, I worked in Professor McKinney's lab investigating *Mycobacteria*, antibiotic resistance, and atomic force microscopy. All of these experiences allowed me not only travel abroad and meet new people, but also familiarize with high-tech lab techniques and equipment.

So where do I start with my experience in the lab? Well, the first thing that you need to remember is that lab equipment and chemical reagents aren't only delicate and require great care, but are also quite expensive. So if you're not so coordinated, you may break or spill things easily. Oops! Believe how much my hands were shaking when I was working with a cryostat worth $15,000.00. This constant fear of touching expensive things may significantly affect your quality of life in the lab. Additionally, experiments usually fail for no apparent reason. You put hours, days, and weeks into your work and in the end, everything fails. This constant uncertainty of whether your experiment will work or not really puts a lot of pressure on you as an intern. Oh, and if you work in a lab with freaking cell lines, you'll need to take care of them on a regular basis regardless of your weekend plans. In other words, forget about a vivacious social life while you're doing your experiments! To survive through your placement, I've made a short list of survival tips. Let's see how you can get ready.

1 Focus on theoretical knowledge

Yes, you need to build your theoretical knowledge of biology to the level of a first-year or second-year undergraduate. A general biology book will suffice. If you get an internship, the last thing you want is to realize that you have no clue what gel electrophoresis is or why sodium dodecyl sulphate (SDS) is used for polyacrylamide gel electrophoresis (PAGE). When you're on your placement, ask your supervisor to recommend you a good book that covers the basics of what your experiment involves (actually, this is a good way to start bonding with your supervisor).

2 Be ready to fail

This is one of the reasons I don't quite like research. It's so unpredictable. It takes a ton of time and effort to do an experiment and still it fails in many cases. So you just need to accept it and persevere. However, even the smallest chance of success may be all that you need to make those long days, sleepless nights, failed experiments, and monotonous lab work worth it in the end. Don't give up. Ever.

3 Don't be too optimistic about your supervisor

I mentioned already that scientists are a particularly busy species of organisms. The reality is that you're going to be a pain in the butt for them. Let's put this straight - don't expect too much! In the majority of cases, you'll be struggling in the lab with a pipette, juggling eppendorfs, or messing about with a PCR machine all on your *own*. Don't expect to be supervised all the time. Be bold and take initiative, but seek assistance from lab technicians if you're unsure. There will probably be some PhD or MSc students around so ask for help from them as they are known for being a friendlier lab species.

4 Show your interest

I'm very interested in personal development and strategies on how to become a better person (no, biology isn't the only subject I'm passionate about). My most favorite author, Dale Carnegie, in his book, '*How To Win Friends & Influence People*', has suggested one strategy which will help make other people like you. It's to become genuinely interested in other people. So when you're on a break with your supervisor and lab mates, ask them about their work, their achievements, and their goals. Be a good listener and appreciate what they have done so far. Make them feel like you are truly and sincerely fascinated by their work. Praise them and honestly express your desire to be like them. If your supervisor is your idol, tell them this directly. Not everyone can read your mind.

5 Be curious no matter how much you hate the subject

When you're in the lab, stay curious and show your interest in everything you're being taught. Raise questions, be inquisitive, and think outside of the box. You see, all these famous scientists possess such qualities. Because you are a budding scientist (aren't you?), this is your time to develop these skills and put them into practice. Even if you find something you don't like, set a positive mindset and just be cheerful. Sincerely. With no mimicries. It worked for me really well. I didn't like so many things in the lab when I was on my placement. But I kept my eyes open all the time, and every single day I tried to find a fascinating detail in unfascinating things. And on the last day of my placement, my supervisor told me I was the most passionate person in the lab throughout the summer. How come? No matter how much you don't like something, stay positive.

6 Make sure you understand the experiment before you do it

Don't pretend to be the master of everything. The lab isn't a good place to impress someone, got it? Before you start the experiment, listen carefully to the instructions that you have to follow. Read the protocol and analyze all the diagrams and illustrations. If you are unsure - STOP and ask for help. Proceed only when it's safe to do so and there is someone around you to help you out in case something goes terribly bad.

7 Wear the right type of protective clothing and gear

Wearing proper clothes and gear in the lab will keep you safe and protected. Don't underestimate the importance of gloves or washing your hands regularly and meticulously. I've heard many supervisors and PhDs saying, *"I've developed a resistance to ethidium bromide"* But you should take all precautions and ignore what others say. It's your health after all.

Don't wear open-toed shoes or shorts in the lab. Remove any loose clothing or jewelry as you aren't on a catwalk. If you have long hair, tie it back. Always wear a lab coat (and wash it regularly or have several spare ones), gloves, a face mask (if needed), and safety goggles when doing experiments or handling chemicals. Be aware of where you can find emergency eye-washers, emergency showers, exhaust hoods, fire blankets, and fire extinguishers so that you can react quickly if something happens.

8 Keep a lab book

From the first day, record everything you do. Use sticky notes if needed and be organized with your lab book. Don't rely on your memory as it'll probably screw you over when you need it most. I did rely a lot on my memory and it failed me almost every single time. See, distractions are all over the place. There's always some noise in the lab as people come and go. And sometimes they stop by, wanting to talk to you (and of course interrupt your experiment). So to avoid any mistakes, document everything on a paper. No matter how trivial your experiment is. Maybe, by a very very improbable chance, you'll make a ground shaking discovery during your placement and you'll need to replicate it to show its validity!

I hope that this section didn't deter you from research and hunting for summer placements. After all, it's all about gaining lab experience and building networks. It's also fun to work in the scientific environment as you build some personal skills like time management and communication with senior staff, too. Most importantly, you learn to fail. Sometimes failures propel you forward, but sometimes they can stop you. So how do you deal with them?

25 HOW TO DEAL WITH FAILURES

**"Our greatest glory is not in never failing,
but in rising every time we fail."**
Confucius

Yes, failing sucks. Probably nothing sucks more than losing after putting in so much effort. And I can tell you from my own experience, it's really painful. But… after many unsuccessful attempts, you'll hit the sweet point. I bet you've heard a very famous saying that we learn more from our failures than from our successes and believe me it is sooo true. All successful people have one thing in common - they fail many times before they finally identify how to succeed. Can you think of any of the greatest achievers who experienced colossal failures? Let me give you some examples.

For instance, Thomas Edison failed thousands of times while trying to invent the light bulb. He said, "*I have found 10,000 ways something won't work. I am not discouraged, because every wrong attempt discarded is another step forward.*" Did you know that Walt Disney was fired from his newspaper job because he "*lacked imagination and good ideas*"? The Wright brothers had to overcome millions of failures while they were creating the first aircraft prototype. The key to their success was to learn from their mistakes, which lead to the discovery that changed the lives of billions: a heavier-than-air powered aircraft that could get airborne and stay there. A famous British politician, Winston Churchill, failed sixth grade and guess what? He was considered "*a dolt*" by his teachers. Later, it turned out he would be the one to lead Britain to victory in the Second World War.

Despite all of these examples, many of us still fear those failures. And if we confront them, we usually allow them to dictate our destiny and, most likely, we'll let them drag us down and leave us defeated. How many of us realize that the word **FAIL** itself is an acronym for First

Attempt In Life? So why are we so scared of first attempts? How can we keep failures from derailing us? How can we let go and move on? Let me propose some steps you can take.

1 Don't take it personally

How many times have you blamed yourself for failures? How many times have you thought that you're dumb? Worthless? Incompetent? When we fail (especially in the biology olympiad), we always tend to blame ourselves. Just because you haven't found the right technique to prepare for the olympiad or haven't learned everything from your textbooks yet doesn't mean that *you* are a failure. So stop personalizing your failures as this can wreak havoc on your confidence and mental state. How? Be bold. Be the boss of your own success. Refuse to let your failures define you. Try again. And fail again. But this time fail harder to achieve greatness.

2 Learn from your failures

For me, failures give me time to breathe, to re-define my values, and to think about how I would do something smarter next time. In the section 'Surviving in the Lab', I was trying to convince you that you'll fail many times in the lab. In fact, scientists fail in their experiments most of the time. But do you think that means they've wasted their time? Definitely not. It means that they've learnt something new that will help them get closer to their objectives.

When you fail, analyze curiously why you failed. Was the failure absolutely beyond your control? Was it because of a lack of time? Resources? Support? Passion? Dedication? Or maybe it was because of laziness? Friends? Weather? Mood? What might you have done differently to get better results? Your failure is a story of what you *shouldn't* do again. So do read this story carefully. Then, take a piece of paper and write everything down (i.e. make your thoughts tangible).

Can you think of what you've learned from your mistakes? If the answer is yes, make a list of things you'd do differently next time. There's no rush to answer all those questions now. See, the answers may take a day or even a week to pop up, so be patient. Once you've thought everything through, make a small plan for how you're going to move forward. Split your plan up into small achievable steps. Take action on just one of them at a time. The important thing is to keep moving forward again. Make the failure your inspiration. Your motivation. Your teacher. Your light, showing the way out.

3 Change negative emotions to positive ones

It's human nature to become emotional when it comes to failures. It's OK to feel moody, pessimistic, and down for a day or week but no more. Let me give you a biological analogy.

Have you ever seen a lion crying over a failed attempt to capture a prey? Or a frustrated peacock after failed mating? Why not? Because there's no evolutionary benefit (or reason) to letting emotions overtake your sanity. It won't change anything. You fail, you smile, and then go forward. So replace feelings of anger, frustration, blame, or regret with optimism. Discard thoughts like, "*I failed, so it means I'm stupid and incapable,*" and embrace a new way of thinking like, "*I failed and now I'm smarter as I know what **not** to do.*" Be persistent and continue with your efforts. This will build strong character, and success will come. Don't expect this to be fast, though. Just like a robust immune response takes time to develop, success takes time to find its way to you.

4 Ignore the insincere opinions of others

We're always surrounded by others. And stupidly enough, their opinion is very (sometimes overly) important to us. Let's be honest! Every single one of us fears being judged by friends, family members, and even random strangers. People gossip. People judge. People hurt. Yes, but should you let that affect your life in any way? It's not a secret that we're especially susceptible to what people say about us when we're young. And there's nothing wrong with that at all. In fact, we strive to nurture others' respect and esteem all the time because this is what helps us get better marks in school, a better job, or more friends. Oh, how wrong this is! It's *your* life. First, flush that fear of not meeting others' expectations down the toilet. Then, listen to what others say but don't let their opinion shape who *you* are. Why? They can do this intentionally to douse your passion, which will consequently undermine your ability to succeed. Additionally, they might just be trying to hide their own failures and insecurities. So to make themselves feel better, they purposefully make your failures look bigger than they actually are.

At the same time, don't isolate yourself, and keep an eye on the feedback you're getting from the environment because you're an open system. Record the external cues but only to stay aware of where you're going. The worst thing you can do is to let them maneuver you away from your goal. Let your successes and failures, not the opinions of others, lead the way. Your way.

5 Don't dwell on your failure for too long

Make it a strict rule to only mourn your failure for less than seven days (one day is ideal). No more. Obsessing over your failures won't change anything and will only trap you in an emotional doom-loop. Can you change the past? What about the future? I hope you see my point. The quicker you put your failures behind you and move on, the quicker your scars become your armor. And don't forget that failure just means you need more practice and possibly a change in your approach. So focus on those two things rather than pitying yourself for what went wrong.

6 Don't bottle it up inside

I know it's very hard to open up, especially if you're an introvert. In fact, I keep everything to myself and I can't cry my heart out to anyone. But believe me, that's not very healthy. Emotions build up little by little and, one day, everything you've stashed deep in your heart may erupt like lava from a quiet volcano. Keep your heart half filled with those emotions and let the other half out into the light. How? The easiest way is by talking about hardships and failures with someone. The bonus is that talking to someone may help you find a way forward or at least inspire you to do something differently in the future.

For some, it's better to open up to someone close but I personally prefer to talk to someone I don't know. Why? By venting about it you can release that inner pressure without being judged by previous prejudices. I really love talking to older people (when I was 19, I worked in a care home and later in a hospital, where I met the most amazing 90-year-olds who helped me learn to look at the world from a different perspective). A person of your age may not be able to understand your struggles, so find someone who is experienced and who has been through many hardships.

7 Put yourself in situations similar to past failures

"No way, I'm not doing this again." I'm guessing that's what you're thinking. Think again. You can't be successful without risk. Just because you made a mistake already doesn't mean you should hide from your past like a planarian hides from the light. You've already had time to analyze what went wrong and what you would do differently next time. Now, it's time to put all that you've learned into practice. Toss your fear aside. This time you'll be armed with the knowledge you need to succeed. So keep trying. Again and again.

8 Focus on your end goal all the time

In the section 'Motivation', we agreed that you'll start your biology olympiad preparation by stating clearly what your ultimate goal is. Did you think you were going to glide effortlessly to success? Trust me, you're going to face competition, failure, jealousy, dishonesty, and cheating, over and over again. And thankfully, relentless motivation builds a thick skin towards any future failures. How do you stay motivated? Turn your attention back to your ultimate goal. It's by far the most effective defense against the excruciating sting of failure. Keep your eyes on the light at the end of the tunnel, not on some random shadows around you. Remind yourself of your goal. Every. Single. Day.

One more thing - you don't need to tell people about your goal. Why on earth would you need their approval or disapproval? Pursue your goals on your own, not for cheers from the crowd. And this will help you avoid all those people who say *"I told you it would never work"* when you make a mistake.

9 Try something new

It's rather comforting to stick to old habits and familiar actions. If you want to overcome a failure, you must be willing to try something new. New risks and new failures will keep you moving away from mediocrity. I'm sure you aren't the one who doesn't enjoy a dash of challenge, are you? Develop a laser sharp focus and seek out new challenges to build resilience and fortitude. Maybe now it's the biology olympiad, but you could try another competition like a chemistry or physics olympiad. Or even something completely unrelated to science like a sports contest.

10 Forget about "I can't"

How many times has a failure made you think you *can't* do something anymore? One? Two? Every time? Let's now imagine this: what if the little chubby baby who is trying to learn how to walk fell once and said to himself, *"That's it. Clearly, I wasn't born to walk. I give up."* How many times after your piano classes have you thought, *"Oh I just wasn't made for music"*? How many times were you rejected by a crush and the only thought that was running through your head was, *"That's it, love just isn't for me"*? Whoa! If we thought in that way every time we failed, do you think we would have ever become who we are today?

The only problem I can see here is that once we confront the failure, we think we can't do anything. To say is always easier than to do. But what if you ditch *"I can't"* and just start going? Failure is thinking you can't when you can. And I know you can. So don't think you can't. Ever. It just doesn't work like that (remember the baby example!).

11 Learn to compartmentalize

Just like cells have many metabolic reactions taking place in different compartments, isolate your failure from the rest of your thoughts. Never let an academic failure have an impact on your personal life (e.g., your relationship with your family or friends) and vice versa. You can't afford to let your failures in one area hamper success in the other areas. A typical example is when you fail in the test, you start quarrels with your parents just because of your bad mood. Compartmentalize your thoughts! Keep them apart and don't let them overtake your entire cerebrum.

12 Look at the failures of others

Now stop and think about whether you're the only person on the planet to face failure. Do you think yours are the biggest? The most painful? Most likely not. Also, usually we look at the success of our friends, relatives, and famous people with so much fascination that we forget to realize that in reality these people encounter failure just as much as anyone else. For example, a famous British writer, J.K. Rowling, was rejected by 12 publishers. Later, her *Harry Potter* series sold over 100 million copies. Can you imagine what would have happened if she had given up after her fifth or tenth attempt? So explore the world carefully and look at the examples of failed attempts around you. Check out blogs and magazines. Also, listen to the speeches of successful people on TED. Successful people appreciate how important it's to embrace the failure and learn from it. So they're in the position to give you honest advice. Remember that you're not alone. Failure is OK.

13 It's all about the journey

We tend to see our lives and everything that happens to or around us in terms of achievement and failure. Achievement usually means we're right, we're good. Failure means we're wrong, we're incapable. If you view your journey towards the biology olympiad as either a success or failure, sorry mate, but you've already failed. You've lost it. The thing is that truly successful people care only about the knowledge of their craft, and they're willing to do whatever it takes to gain it. You can't make a complete map without going off the beaten path, getting lost, and then coming back and putting what you've found on paper. You try, you fail, and you discover a different way of doing things without "failing" along the journey. See, birth takes about eight hours and death takes a bit less than a few minutes but a person's lifetime can span many decades. So it's not about the start or the finish. It's about the *journey* in between. Making many mistakes during your journey isn't a bad thing. But making the same mistake many times is detrimental.

If you want to grow as a biologist, you have to aim outside of your comfort zone and push yourself hard to stretch for things you want. For me, I feel that without failing, success isn't worth it. So learn to fail. Make mistakes. Keep failing until you fail to fail. And bingo! You cracked the code. Enjoy the journey and remember that more good has come from mistakes than from successes.

26 MY EXPERIENCE IN BIOLOGY OLYMPIADS

"Do not go where the path may lead,
go instead where there is no path
and leave a trail."
Ralph Waldo Emerson

I started my biology olympiad journey in 2010. Back in 2009, I was accepted to the best school in Lithuania and, not surprisingly, a staggering number of students from this school tend to participate in the national and international olympiads and competitions. In fact, many of such students won gold, silver, and bronze medals in the international olympiads and then went on to study at the best universities in the world. For this very reason, teachers and pupils were always whispering about these olympiad geniuses in my new school. I soon learned about two girls from a senior grade who recently took part in the IBO and I managed to meet them in person. Guess what? They inspired me so much by their knowledge and intelligence, so it didn't take long before I got the bible of biology, the textbook (a.k.a. Campbible).

It took me a lot of time to prepare. Honestly, I intentionally skipped school, and if I was at school I always had my biology notes under my math or English books. I also signed up for a genetics club at the local university where I learned some crucial lab techniques. Moreover, in Lithuania we had an awesome initiative led by the university students called *'BioSa'*. What these guys did was to organize weekly online biology tests, and the best performers were invited to monthly or bimonthly three-day workshops at the best universities in Lithuania. In these practical workshops, I learned to dissect various animals (**Figure 11**), recognize and classify different insects, run gel electrophoresis, and make plant stem and root cross sections. I also met incredible people who remain some of my best friends to this day.

Figure 11 Dissection Of A Fish During One Of The 'BioSa' Workshops

I was lucky enough to represent Lithuania in two IBOs, one in 2012 (Singapore) and one in 2013 (Switzerland), both times winning a bronze medal (mainly due to my really, really bad performance in practicals). My results compared to the 1st place results are shown in **Table 12** and **Table 13**. As you can see, I screwed up quite a lot and you might be wondering why on earth I'm writing this book. Frankly speaking, I'm not sure why. But, just thinking out loud, do you think you can learn more from success than from mistakes? So often, when I look back on my olympiad preparation, I can see that all the failures actually paved the way for something far better. They catalyzed my desire to learn more and share my knowledge with others. That's why I set up Biolympiads.com back in 2014. I chose the way without a path (do you remember the quote at the beginning?) because I want to ignite that tiny spark of motivation in *you* to work hard and learn and of course leave a narrow trail in the biology olympiad forest. And you know what? That's what actually sets me apart from others - I wasn't great then, but I didn't give up and continued learning.

Table 12 My Results In The IBO 2012 Olympiad

| Rank | Name | Theory | | | Practicals | | | | |
		Th 1	Th 2	Total	P1	P2	P3	P4	Total
1	xxxxx	76	78.45	154.45	91	69.5	83.4	89.5	333.4
80	Martyna Petrulyte	64.9	61.4	126.3	67	35.5	71.1	67.3	240.9

Coming back to my IBO experience, it was the best time I've ever had. Singapore was one of the first countries that I visited outside of Europe and Switzerland was one of the first countries I visited in Europe. The best thing about olympiads is that you get a paid holiday abroad, you meet people from *all* over the world, and you get to know different and unique cultures. Besides, you take the most unique exam papers in the entire world, which are hard to solve even for experienced scientists.

Let me start with my experience in Singapore. We arrived there a few days before the official start to get used to the time difference and also to get acquainted with the country itself. It was my first time coming to a country with tropical weather. The heat, the monsoon rains, and the humidity were all so hard to bear. However, flora and fauna made up for the uncomfortable climate. It was especially impressive to hear cicadas singing in the middle of the city and to see unique creatures crawling on the pavements. While exploring the city, we visited the famous retail stretch of Orchard Road, which is cramped with chic shopping centres. It's not a secret that Singaporeans are mad for shopping so it was fascinating to see what kind of stuff they buy. While walking around, we found out that cars in Singapore are very expensive and thus the public transportation system is well developed.

Table 13 My Results In The IBO 2013 Olympiad

Rank	Name	Theory			Practicals				
		Th 1	Th 2	Total	P1	P2	P3	P4	Total
1	xxxxx	37	37.8	74.8	64.8	65.5	66.75	82.344	279.394
74	Martyna Petrulyte	23.4	31.2	54.6	66.6	58.5	60.5	78.17	263.77

The 23rd IBO began with an outstanding performance by an orchestra and Singaporean dancers (**Figure 12**) and the opening ceremony was graced by a talk from the President of the Republic of Singapore. After that, we discovered the amazing cuisine of Singapore. We had an opportunity to taste food ranging from Malaysian stir-fry chicken to Indian curries to Chinese noodles. There is probably no national dish in this country because their cuisine is a mixture of cultures but the food is quite cheap and of good quality so there is no need for fancy restaurants or outstanding chefs to explore the authenticity and taste of the dishes. One thing that I didn't fall in love with was durians, the famous stinky fruit which Singaporeans adore. How on earth can you eat something that tastes like an onion for dessert? Oh, and it has such a bad smell that you can get a fine if you take durians on public transportation.

Figure 12 The Opening Ceremony At The IBO 2013.

The next day we had a six-hour practical examination and the day after that an adrenaline-filled six-hour long theoretical exam. We had Animal Anatomy and Ecology (**Figure 13**), Microbiology and Biochemistry, Cell and Molecular Biology practicals, and, last but not least, a Plant Diversity, Anatomy, and Physiology practical. The theory exam was very mind-numbing and challenging. Fortunately, after an exhausting day we had a fabulous Bhangra Extravaganza and an indian-themed buffet dinner. Everyone, including students, jury members, and the organizing committee, were dancing vigorously along with the performers on stage, partying our hearts out!

The next day we had lots of excursions and social events. We visited the Jurong Bird Park which is one of the most renowned bird sanctuaries with some of the largest free-flying aviaries in the world. We watched a stunning visual fiesta of performances on stage by birds of different species, from pelicans to flamingos and hornbills. The last stop that day was a visit to the NEWater plant where we got an insight into how Singapore employs innovative technologies to recycle water. The guided factory tour was definitely eye-opening and we all promised from that day on to conserve our precious water.

We also went to the Singapore Zoo park, which is among the most beautiful wildlife park settings in the world where animals roam freely in the open and naturalistic habitats. What's more, we enjoyed visiting the Underwater World at Sentosa where we were engaged with majestic sharks and rays, exotic Sea Dragons, ethereal Sea Angels, and living fossils like the Arapaima. A kite-making workshop brought students together with mentors, as well as organizers, to exchange experiences, ideas, and knowledge. I was really astounded by the hospitality of the country and by the very kind and happy people of various backgrounds living together as one big family in such a tiny country.

Figure 13 A Zoology Practical In The Biology Olympiad

The IBO 2013 in Bern wasn't as special to me as it took place in Europe, where I live. The same weather, the same food, and quite the same culture. Nevertheless, I had a great time meeting old and new friends with whom I get in touch with every so often, even after such a long time.

The opening ceremony was filled with authentic Swiss performances as well as the sounds of different languages. Moreover, many students wore their national attire and it was fascinating to see them in their fancy dresses and suits. It became a tradition for every country to bring some small gifts for other participants, and so in the ceremony we exchanged little gifts with fellow participants. Now one of my desk drawers is full of pencils, small Mongolian yurts, fans, and other cute things from the IBO.

After our arrival, we were introduced to our team guide, who was a local university student. During the olympiad in Bern, we stayed in a hotel with all the other participants.

Figure 14 Me And My Fellow Team Members Enjoying The Beautiful Scenery Of Switzerland At The IBO 2013

During the first few days we took a series of practical (lasting for six hours which included Comparative and Functional Biosystematics, Molecular Cell Biology, Plant Ecology and Physiology and Evolutionary Ethology) and theoretical exams. For the first time in the theoretical exam there were no papers and we had to answer multiple-choice questions on tablets. This was very state-of-the-art but there were many problems with the test system. The connection was slow, the questions weren't loading fast - honestly, I wasted so much time just trying to solve those IT problems. Furthermore, we used digital technology during one of the practical exams, the Evolutionary Ethology practical, and saw how experiments are performed, how to analyze the results, as well as how to draw scientific inferences using the latest technologies.

After the theoretical exams, we were treated to a dinner full of dishes made with Swiss or Liechtenstein specialities, for example, raclette (melted cheese with potatoes) and vermicelles (chestnut purée). After the meal, we had an opportunity to attend several Swiss workshops. At the Alphorn workshop, we could try playing a traditional instrument which is essentially a labrophone that consists of a several-meters-long, straight, natural wooden horn of a conical bore. The Swiss-German workshop helped us learn some words of the language spoken in Switzerland. A chocolate workshop followed and attracted the most people where we could try decorating chocolate and even got to take our creations home.

On the other days we had the opportunity to get to know each other and explore Switzerland. We went on impressive excursions to Lake Thun where there was mind-blowing scenery, Niederhorn Mountain in the Bernese Alps (**Figure 14**), and the St. Beatus Caves. The sights were simply breathtaking. The last part of the trip was a visit to a cheese dairy in

Affoltern, where we learned about the art of cheese-making and had a chance to taste different Swiss cheeses. We also went on a guided tour around Bern. During the tour, we took pictures of panoramic views from the "Bundeshaus" (Parliament) of the "Münster" (Cathedral), the "Zytglogge" (Clock Tower), a medieval astronomical clock in the center of Bern, and of the Rose Garden, where our tour ended. Believe me, the tidiness of the city surprised everyone. After the Bundeshaus visit, we changed into our white lab coats and flooded into the Bundesplatz for the main event: "Biology Around the World: Meet Our Guests", which was a flash mob type of event.

I can tell you without a single doubt that the IBO (the two of them, actually) changed my life. The olympiad will rarely earn you fame and glory but it'll affect you and your future in many other ways. So work hard and chase your dreams so that the upcoming IBO changes your life, too!

27 BEYOND THE BIOLOGY OLYMPIAD

"The time to be happy is now.
The place to be happy is here.
The way to be happy is to make others so."
Robert Green Ingersoll

One of the key reasons why so many students want to participate in the biology olympiad is that the experience is a great item to have on their CV. Imagine you got an award, and you were almost guaranteed a place at a top university. Some universities can actually exempt you from taking the entrance examination if you have a medal from the IBO. I know how daunting it's to get into the best college or university. And high competition for a limited number of places at universities as well as strict requirements for the applications don't help either. So how do you get into the university you have always been dreaming of?

You need to first decide on which university or college you want to go to. Parents play a huge role in deciding where you'll eventually apply, no? Most likely, they want you to go to the "big name" colleges like Harvard, Yale, Princeton or Stanford in the USA or Cambridge and Oxford in the UK, to name a few. While various university rankings may affect your ultimate university choice, remember that it's all about *your* preferences, *your* feelings, and wishes. Before applying to universities, do your thorough research. Investigate every single university like Sherlock Holmes: collect proof and dig up all the facts about the university you wish to apply to. Look carefully at what they have to offer you with regards to academics, social life, facilities, and extracurricular activities.

Admittedly, the most important thing you have to consider is academics. Does the university or college offer the degree program you want to pursue? Do you prefer informative lectures or problem-based learning and lively discussions? Are you more into hands-on research or theoretical approaches? Look up who works in the department and consider if their academic experience matches your aspirations. Carefully review the curriculum of the entire course. Trust me, it's super important. I didn't do this and was thus in agony during my fourth year at the university. Why? I found out far too late that I'd be doing a Developmental Biology course. Oh and believe me, I really don't like all these germ layers, involutions and, for example, how the eye develops from the optic vesicle. Make sure everything in the program satisfies you to avoid disappointment later.

Next, think about geography. Do you enjoy year-round sunshine and high vitamin D levels, or do you prefer the winter season more? Perhaps you dream of writing your assignments and essays in the shadow of the Eiffel Tower, or maybe you would like to stay at home (which would be very comfortable and cheap as you wouldn't need to think about food and rent). Your life after school isn't only about education but also about the journey, so consider carefully what type of location you love the most. For instance, I don't like the sun and hot weather, so I chose a university in Scotland.

The ambience of the surroundings also plays a role in your university choice. Perhaps you can't live in a city without a buzzing nightlife. Or if you're into nature and yearn for grassy fields and open spaces, you might go rural. What about the size of the school? Universities come in all possible sizes so think about whether you like being in tiny places where everybody knows everybody or if you prefer being anonymous in a large crowd of students. Remember that bigger colleges and universities usually have a large campus and lots of different things to do. In contrast, smaller universities may be more individual-oriented, intimate, and personal. Additionally, figure out the distance you would walk every day to lectures and your means of transportation. Can you afford paying for public transport? Would you buy a bike? All these little details will affect your final decision.

Here's the most important part. Think about the cost of tuition, any scholarships and financial aid you can get from your prospective college or university. Public universities are much cheaper but private ones might offer some privately-funded scholarships, so don't be deterred by the initial high price tag. Furthermore, if you're a foreign student, there might be many difficulties, not to mention having to pay much higher international student fees. Also read carefully about visa requirements. Check if there are any scholarships for those with special talents outside of the classroom, like athletes or musicians. Don't forget to take into account extra expenses like housing, food, books, and any leisure activities like the gym.

Another crucial point to investigate is whether there are any exchange programs available. Trust me, international experience may mature your personality in like a month or two and you might become a completely different person (been there, became one). I left Lithuania and went on to complete my BSc degree in Biomedical Sciences in the UK at the age of 19. Then, I spent one summer in Israel and the next one in Switzerland. After graduation, I moved to Malta. These experiences equipped me with life skills like empathy, adaptability, flexibility and problem-solving, and in few years I became a well-adjusted and self-aware person. And think about the benefits of learning a new language. I know it's very comfortable to stay in your country, but don't be afraid to go out of your comfort zone and change your life. Think about all the amazing people you'll meet, places you'll see, food you'll eat, and skills you'll develop. Do you think you'll have time to travel after graduation? Sadly, you're wrong. You'll be pressured by big loans, and everyone will be telling you to find a job ASAP. When you're in such a situation, you probably won't have either the time nor the money to travel.

Another useful thing to do before you make a decision is to ask friends who attend university for advice. Then, formulate your own opinion based on these facts. It might be worth going to an open day or at least on a tour around the campus. Sometimes, when you see the campus and the facilities, you'll get a "meh" feeling. But other times, you might feel like you're at home. Concerning which university or college to pick, you need to follow your gut. Don't let your own opinion and feelings become clouded by anyone else's. It's *you* who will be spending the next three to four years there, not your parents or friends, so choose whatever feels right for *you*.

When you've made your decision, the next thing to think about is your personal statement. Dedicate enough time to craft the perfect letter that clearly demonstrates your suitability and passion for your chosen field of study. You might be wondering what to put in the personal statement. To begin with, you'll most certainly need to explain why you want to attend that particular university or college. Honestly explain what attracted you and don't be too vague. Don't just say, "*I love the location of the campus*," but instead explain what's so good about the location (maybe it is its proximity to your favorite café or maybe because it's close to the park and being close to nature helps you learn faster). Then think about what makes you suitable for the program you're applying for. Can you give any examples of relevant skills and experience you've gained from your education, paid or voluntary work, or any extracurricular activities?

When you say you have a particular skill, explain how you gained it. For instance, rather than simply stating that you are academically astute and clever, give real examples from your career in the biology olympiads and in the lab doing a science project. Don't just boast about your achievements in the olympiad (e.g., "*I won X number of gold medals*"), but mention what transferable skills you acquired and, importantly, how they'll benefit the community of the college or university. Think about what you can give. Stand out from the crowd by highlighting your collaborative spirit and tell the reader what you've done so far for your school's community. It might be, for instance, tutoring, which allowed you to develop leadership skills and become a good team player. In general, forget about yourself and think about how you'll make college life better for *others*. Simple as that. If, however, you haven't been successful in the olympiad, appreciate this and explain that it enabled you to experience failure without any repercussions. It actually taught you to deal with the let-downs which are a normal part of life. After all, who doesn't like a humble self-evaluation?

Don't forget to include a paragraph about any clubs or societies you are a member of, any employment or volunteering that you've done, any summer schools or courses that you've attended, or online courses you've completed. Highlight what skills you gained and exemplify this with any real-life situations where you put those skills into practice. Most importantly, make your interest and enthusiasm clear! Tell them in your letter what your ultimate goal is and how that particular degree will help you achieve your aims.

To recap, begin your personal statement by explaining what attracted you to that university and that program. Then move on to explain how your academic and extracurricular experience has prepared you for the course. Exemplify your skills with situations where you demonstrated those skills. End with a paragraph which explains your ultimate goal (*"I want to become a world-famous scientist"* won't take you far as it's too shallow), commitment, and interest in the course. State clearly how that degree will help you achieve your aim. Needless to say, it's all about *others* and the wider community as far as the university application is concerned. So think hard what you want to do in your university life for others.

28 ONLY FOR TEACHERS

*"He who dares to teach
must never cease to learn."*
Richard Henry Dann

So it might very well be that you're a science or biology teacher and you're reading this book with the aim of finding some tips on how to help your pupils prepare for the biology olympiad. Or maybe you are looking for inspiration to start administering the olympiad at your school. It doesn't matter what reason brought you here, but before we begin I really want to thank you for what you're doing. You believe (and I believe) that a biology olympiad is important and that it can really be a life-changer. Not only for the student, but for you too. How come? Imagine how you would feel if the person you prepared for the olympiad gets into the best college or university, and achieved this because of you. Imagine what it would be like to tutor someone who one day will cure deadly diseases or discover new things that will change the lives of millions. I don't know about you, but for me helping someone reach their dreams is the best reward I could possibly get. This realization, that *you* have made a difference in someone's life, is what drives me forward and is what actually drove me to write this book.

Working with students who have the capacity to learn more at a faster rate than is typical for their peers is a colossal challenge for any teacher. I'm guessing you know a lot of bright students in your classroom who could potentially take part in the biology olympiad. Before you start recruiting them for the contest, you need to understand that the preparation for the biology olympiad is very different from the preparation for a standard school exam. Believe me, it's quite a big challenge both for you and your students.

The olympiad curriculum will go far beyond the facts. It'll cover biology in greater breadth and depth as well as include more difficult biological concepts. What's more, it'll encourage you and your students to delve into new ideas and use your knowledge to analyze, evaluate, and solve problems. How? The exam format is put together in such a way that it differentiates between average and exceptional students.

Test items are typically multiple choice or multiple response (True/False) type. And the questions may contain descriptions, figures, graphs, tables, and results of experimental data which means that students need to develop analytical and critical thinking skills. With this in mind, the preparation should be focused on developing students to equip them with such skills.

Unfortunately, there aren't many resources designed just for the olympiad. Annoying, isn't it? Regardless, you can help your students in many ways. First, find out any requirements for registration for the local biology olympiad and make sure that your school is eligible to take part. In some countries there is a fee for schools so check this out and get all the necessary approvals from your superiors. Then, recruit students using different channels (e.g., announcements in the classroom, posters, fliers, and email communication etc.). The next step is to plan how you're going to prepare your students for the contest. Think about what resources, speakers, practice sessions, and lab practicals you'll use to aid learning. Are there any resources in your school like textbooks and lab equipment already? Do you have a budget for any additional costs? Think about these things well in advance to avoid any issues later. Check out **Table 14** for more tips.

Hopefully this will get you going. Just remember you're not alone in this daunting journey - trillions of bacteria are on you and in you at all times (in fact, bacteria is the only culture some people have!). And if you still need some more help, turn to fellow teachers and past olympiad participants from your school. I'm sure they'll be happy to help.

Table 14 Tips On How To Help Your Students Prepare For The Biology Olympiad

What?	How?
Help students fully understand the depth, breadth, and rigor of the exams	Provide practice questions, solve and analyze past papers together to understand the format of the test and how to approach the questions. Visit the IBO site (www.ibo-info.org) to obtain an overview of the IBO competition as national olympiads are structured similarly.
Help students gain theoretical knowledge	Provide a list of reference textbooks (one for each big biology topic: Animal Anatomy and Physiology, Cell Biology, Genetics and Evolution, Plant Anatomy and Physiology, Ecology, plus one general biology textbook - 6 in total. For Ethology and Biosystematics, a general biology textbook is enough).

	Source study guides, presentations, and study notes from the Internet (check the lists in the section 'Must Know Biology Topics'). Arrange regular (weekly or biweekly) biology olympiad preparation meetings during which students will cover all crucial biology topics and practice past papers. MIT OpenCourseWare is another freely available educational resource. The courses may include audios of the lectures, recitations, notes, problem sets, and exams, all of which resemble the biology olympiad. Review these resources with your students as they are problem-solving oriented. Look for biology courses from Coursera.
Continuously check students' progress	Organize weekly or fortnightly mock olympiad exams to check students' progress (for the mocks, you can use biology olympiad past papers).
Help students gain practical skills	Review the practical exams from the IBO and familiarize yourself with the list of techniques from section 'Developing Practical Skills'. Identify what experiments you could do with your students using the resources available in your school. If you have any acquaintances, get in touch with the local university and arrange some training sessions there. Alternatively, you can find all the techniques on the Internet and watch how they are performed together with your students.
Inspire and motivate your students	Praise students for their courage and passion. Encourage and appreciate their efforts. Discuss any uncertainties as students may be intimidated and discouraged by the difficulty of the exam. Organize regular meetups and lunches/dinners to foster team spirit and build a community. Make sure everyone turns up. Try to get a scholarship for the winner of the olympiad to further encourage students. Invite some scientists to the school to inspire teenagers to get into the sciences.

29 TO THE PARENTS

"The best way to make children good is to make them happy."
Oscar Wilde

If you're a parent, this section is for you, moms and dads, who donated egg and sperm, respectively, to your awesome children, because you are role models and inspirations to them. They depend on *you*. They believe in *you*. They trust *you*. And they love *you*. They will turn to you whenever they have any problems or uncertainties. No matter how crazy they become during puberty, you'll be the ones who will give them much needed sanity. That's why I wanted to discuss some things with you to make sure we're all on the same page as far as the biology olympiad is concerned.

Without any further ado, let me ask you this - why did your kid decide to take part in the biology olympiad? Was it because of his or her pure interest in biology? Thirst for challenge? Desire to win a medal? Or is it because of *you*? *Your* desires? *Your* dream for your kid to be the best, smartest, and most astute? The number of people in the world is increasing and competition is becoming more and more fierce, meaning that you, as a parent, must find some way to help your kid stand out from the crowd.

Let's be honest, the overemphasis on getting into the best possible college becomes a serious burden on our teenagers with an interest in biology. They start to feel that they need to do well to make you guys happy. Qualifying for the biology olympiad will definitely help your kid when applying for further studies. And your teenager will definitely develop critical and analytical thinking skills. Lastly, it'll definitely show your son's or daughter's true potential. And let me guess: The biology olympiad isn't the only competition your kid is taking part in. Isn't it because more olympiads mean bigger chances for your child to prove himself or herself, and make you proud? I met parents who saw it as a great honor to themselves if their teenager was successful in many different olympiads. So to encourage their kids to work harder, they put a lot of psychological pressure on their child. I get it, but...

Pause for a moment.

Yes, our kids make us proud because of their academic achievements. But do we pay attention to the fact that their adolescence becomes more stressful and burdened by endless hours of studying and by a ton of books? We literally throw them recklessly into an ocean of peer pressure and competition. And what about the considerable pressure of performing well in these olympiads? If a child has no interest in the subject, do you think this pressure is healthy for their young mind and body? If we're *forcing* our kids to excel in the olympiad, aren't we silently robbing our teenagers of their best years and careless days? Or do you honestly think by forcing your child to compete in the olympiad you'll ignite a passion for science?

I wholeheartedly doubt it. And let me tell you why. All these successful, smart kids that I met in my olympiad career and who won the top medals had one common special sparkling attribute - they were driven by their *own* interest in the subject. I've tutored and prepared many students from all over the world for the olympiad. And trust me, I could tell immediately which ones signed up for the classes because of pure desire to learn and which ones were forced by their parents. Those who study for the olympiad because they just love it were always super excited about every single class, and most importantly they infected me with their excitement, too. All the others had neither passion nor interest. And obviously because of this, they weren't successful in the competition.

Now let's flip the coin and ask ourselves how our high-achieving teenagers react to failure at the olympiad. Unsuccessful participation in the olympiad may make us more confident and determined to succeed the next time. However, some young people take criticism at face value. In this latter case, failure may sink your kid into self-doubt and self-loathing. And what about the pressure from fellow students which may rapidly build up if your child doesn't succeed? Could he or she become the object of bullying? Quite possibly. After all, it takes time and experience to develop the maturity required to realize that a failure occurs not to make us give up, but to give us strength to do better.

Let me tell you this straight: if you really care about your child's success, it's much more important for your child to discover his or her *own* interests rather than to be fed your own or those of society. Motivation is a very personal quality that develops in an inside-out, not outside-in, fashion. So, what makes me love biology may make you loathe it. Thus, I feel that by forcefully enrolling your child into competitive olympiads, you're doing more bad than good. But don't worry, you can change this. How?

First, find ways to enable your child to find his or her passion. It might not be the sciences, math, or any other STEM subject. Perhaps it's arts? Or music? Be understanding and forget about what *you* want - it's your child's life. Let *them* decide what they'll be doing for the rest of their life. Not everyone was born to be a doctor or lawyer, so let them follow their heart. Then, foster the mindset of studying that subject for the joy of it, not as a duty to you or to others. Change your and your child's focus - emphasize the journey and experience, not the destination. Give rewards along the way, not just at the end of the journey. Encourage the pursuit of knowledge, not glory. Finally, realize and embrace the fact that there aren't good or bad students. There are only passionate and disinterested students. The thing I learned during my olympiad preparation is that knowledge is relatively cheap but passion is priceless. If you're lucky enough to find your child's passion, *nurture* it. Every day. And you won't regret it.

The other important thing I wanted to discuss with you is about coping with failures. No parent wants their children to feel bad about themselves and so they ferociously try to protect their kids from any kind of pain of dashed expectations. This is very true for the biology olympiads, too. There is just a limited number of places in the nationals and only four places in the international competition, but there is an ever-increasing number of participants who want to take part in the olympiad. Think about this: what is the probability that a random teenager will turn out to be not only the smartest in the school, but also in the city, country, and possibly in the world? Can you see my point? This means the chances of winning something in the olympiad are shrinking every year. This consequently leads to an increasing number of kids who don't qualify for the next round. Now, you might think that these disappointments are bad, no?

Well, the irony is that such failures in the biology olympiad (and in academic life in general) are actually beneficial for our children. Guess why? You know better than me that learning how to deal with setbacks catalyzes the formation of key life skills they'll need in order to succeed later in their lives. These are emotional resilience and intelligence, self-awareness, coping skills, and optimism.

I met so many families where parents see failure as a source of excruciating pain and not as an opportunity. If you're shaking your head and still holding on to the idea that it's your duty to protect your child from any negative emotion, then the best thing you can do is to determine how much struggling your son or daughter can bear. You see, in biology, extremes on either side are usually bad but moderate amounts of stress or disturbance are best. If philosophy is closer to you than theoretical biology, the definition of the golden mean was deeply rooted in the Greek mentality. Many famous philosophers of that time encouraged people to choose the mean and avoid the extremes on either side. Phocylides, for example, postulated that, "*in many things the middle have the best.*" So how do you find that golden mean? The hack is that you need to be the *guide* for your child, not the savior.

If your child falls short at the olympiad, leave him or her alone for a while. Don't ask *why*, *what*, or *how*. And please don't blame us. Believe me, this annoys teenagers (at least it really pissed me off). In fact, silence is the best weapon you can use to fight treacherous teenage emotions. Give some breathing space to allow your child to analyze the situation, evaluate its seriousness, and come up with some solutions. Instead of saying things, try doing something to help your child cope with the failure. Maybe it's time to find a tutor or mentor. Or maybe you should sign him or her up for a biology summer course or a science club to help them learn more.

Finally, strive to be a good role model for your child. They always watch you like a hawk, so handle your own disappointments in such a way that you would like your kids to handle theirs. Always show healthy coping skills like optimism, determination, and perseverance. We, young people, mimic you, adults. So, give them something *great* to mimic.

30 LINKS

In the book, you saw that I was always referring to **www.Biolympiads.com**. This is the website I set up back in 2014. On it, I share my experience in the biology olympiad, including various tips & tricks. You can also find many study resources and practice problems there.

My newest project, **www.Tutor4Competitions.com**, eats up all my time now. The aim of the website is to connect you guys with past olympiad participants. As you know, it's hard to find someone who specializes in preparing students for the olympiads, and Tutor 4 Competitions solves this problem.

For all guidelines and past papers of the IBO head to **www.IBO-info.org**.

For biology videos, go to **www.KhanAcademy.org**.

For practice problems, go to MIT OpenCourseWare at **https://ocw.mit.edu/index.htm**.

31 FINAL REMARKS

Across the whole world, many people live and breathe biology. I hope after reading this book you got the impression that the olympiad isn't only about knowledge. Frankly, through the ups and downs of the biology olympiad, I've learned more about myself and the world around me than in all of these biology-free years. And guess what the most valuable aspect of the competition was?

No, it wasn't medals, admission letters to the best universities, or glory. To me it was, and always will be, the community built around it. It's all about cooperation and knowledge exchange. All these people from different cultural and academic backgrounds and world-class mentors that I met gave me an eye-opening glimpse of the world beyond my school and my country. This experience made me a citizen of a global community (so far, I've lived in 7 countries and I'm trying to master 6 languages). And obviously, it opened up many diverse career options like medicine, research, and teaching (and writing a book! Yay!).

But you know what gets on my nerves? Yes, a myelin sheath (hahaha...), but also people who are always comparing themselves to others. Have you ever heard someone (or yourself?) saying, *"Oh, they're better than me"*, *"Other kids know more than I do"*, or *"I wish I had a brain like theirs"*? Stop thinking about others. Focus on *yourself*! Become the best version of you! Don't waste your precious ATP trying to live up to what somebody else wants you to be or do. Share the things you learn and inspire others. And please stop looking for a secret trick or a magic recipe to help you prepare for the olympiad. Just start. Anywhere you want. With anything you have. For any time you've got. Follow your passion 24/7. Until the heart stops beating and the lungs stop breathing.

32 REFERENCES

[1] Walker, M.P., Stickgold, R. (2004) Sleep-dependent learning and memory consolidation. Neuron, 44(1):121-33.

[2] Coffield, F., Moseley, D., Hall, E., Ecclestone, K. (2004) Learning Styles and Pedagogy in Post-16 Learning: A Systematic and Critical Review. London: Learning and Skills Research Centre; 84.

[3] Rohrer, D., & Pashler, H. (2012) Learning styles: Where's the evidence? Medical Education, *46*, 630-635.

[4] James, L.E. (2004) Meeting Mr. Farmer versus meeting a farmer: specific effects of aging on learning proper names. Psych Aging 19:515-522.

[5] Naka, M., Naoi, H. (1995) The effect of repeated writing on memory. Mem Cognit. 23(2):201-12.

[6] Bui, D. C., Myerson, J., & Hale, S. (2013) Note-taking with computers: Exploring alternative strategies for improved recall. *Journal of Educational Psychology, 105*(2), 299-309.

[7] Gimenez, P., Bugescu, N., Black, J.M., *et al*. (2014) Neuroimaging correlates of handwriting quality as children learn to read and write. *Frontiers in Human Neuroscience*. 8:155.

[8] Jamesa, K.H., Engelhard, L. (2012) The effects of handwriting experience on functional brain development in pre-literate children. Trends in Neuroscience and Education, Volume 1, Issue 1, Pages 32-42.

[9] Ariga, A., and Lleras, A. (2011). Brief and rare mental "breaks" keep you focused: deactivation and reactivation of task goals pre-empt vigilance decrements. Cognition 118,439 –443.

[10] Payne, J. D., Tucker, M. A., Ellenbogen, J. M., Wamsley, E. J., Walker, M. P., Schacter, D. L., & Stickgold, R. (2012) Memory for Semantically Related and Unrelated Declarative Information: The Benefit of Sleep, the Cost of Wake. PLoS ONE, 7(3), e33079.

[11] Howard, C., Nusbaum,C.H., Uddin, S., Van Hedger, S.C., Heald, S.L.M. (2018) Consolidating skill learning through sleep. Current Opinion in Behavioral Sciences, 20, 174-182.

[12] Chapman, S. B., Aslan, S., Spence, J. S., DeFina, L. F., Keebler, M. W., Didehbani, N., & Lu, H. (2013) Shorter term aerobic exercise improves brain, cognition, and cardiovascular fitness in aging. Frontiers in Aging Neuroscience, 5, 75.

[13] Alfini, A. J., Weiss, L. R., Leitner, B. P., Smith, T. J., Hagberg, J. M., & Smith, J. C. (2016) Hippocampal and Cerebral Blood Flow after Exercise Cessation in Master Athletes. Frontiers in Aging Neuroscience, 8, 184. http://doi.org/10.3389/fnagi.2016.00184

[14] Chellappa, S.L., Ly, J. Q. M., Meyer, C., Balteau, E., Degueldre, C., Luxen, A., Phillips, A., Cooper, H.M. and Vandewalle, G. (2014) Photic memory for executive brain responses. PNAS, DOI: 10.1073/pnas.1320005111.

[15] Amraei, M., Mohamadpour, R., Moayeri, A., Abbasi, N., Shirzadpour, E., Mohamadpour, M. (2017) Vitamin D and its association with memory and learning: A systematic review and meta-analysis. Biomedical Research 2017; 28 (17): 7427-7433.

[16] Cottrell, S. (2006) The Exam Skills Handbook. Basingstoke: Palgrave Macmillan.

[17] Cepeda, N. J., Pashler, H., Vul, E., Wixted, J. T., & Rohrer, D. (2006) Distributed practice in verbal recall tasks: A review and quantitative synthesis. Psychological Bulletin, 132, 354–380.

[18] Forrin, N.D. & MacLeod, C.M. (2017) This time it's personal: the memory benefit of hearing oneself. Memory, 26:4, pp. 574-579.

[19] Howard, C., Nusbaum,C.H., Uddin, S., Van Hedger, S.C., Heald, S.L.M. (2018) Consolidating skill learning through sleep. Current Opinion in Behavioral Sciences, 20, 174-182.

[20] Maier, M. H., (2016) Rotating note taker. College Teaching, 64 (3), 148.

[21] Mueller, P.A., Oppenheimer, D.M. (2014) The pen is mightier than the keyboard: advantages of longhand over laptop note taking. Psychological science, Volume: 25 issue: 6, page(s): 1159-1168.

[22] Dzulkifli, M. A., & Mustafar, M. F. (2013) The Influence of Colour on Memory Performance: A Review. The Malaysian Journal of Medical Sciences : MJMS, 20(2), 3–9.

[23] Morélis, H. (2016) Designing a reliable Theory Test for the International Biology Olympiad, http://www.iboinfo.org/pdf/Designing%20a%20reliable%20IBO%20Theory-HMroct2011.pdf, accessed 23 April 2018.

[24] Stampfer, M.J., Colditz, G.A. (1991) Estrogen replacement therapy and coronary heart disease: a quantitative assessment of the epidemiologic evidence. Prev Med., 20:47–63. doi: 10.1016/0091-7435(91)90006-P.

[25] Lawlor, D.A., Davey Smith, G., Ebrahim, S. (2004) Commentary: the hormone replacement-coronary heart disease conundrum: is this the death of observational epidemiology? Int J Epidemiol., 33(3):464-7. Epub 2004 May 27.

[26] Bloom, B. S., Krathwohl, D. R., Masia, B. B. Taxonomy of Educational Objectives: The Classification of Educational Goals. New York, NY: D. McKay; 1956.

[27] https://www.usabo-trc.org/ [Accessed on 24 March 2018]

[28] Crowe, A., Dirks, C., & Wenderoth, M. P. (2008) Biology in Bloom: Implementing Bloom's Taxonomy to Enhance Student Learning in Biology. CBE Life Sciences Education, 7(4), 368–381.

[29] http://www.ibo-info.org/pdf/20170731%20-%20IBO%20Operational%20Guidelines%20v1.pdf [Accessed on 24 June 2018]

[30] Abedalthagafi, M., Bi, W. L., Aizer, A. A., Merrill, P. H., Brewster, R., Agarwalla, P. K., … Santagata, S. (2016) Oncogenic PI3K mutations are as common as AKT1 and SMO mutations in meningioma. Neuro-Oncology, 18(5), 649–655.

ABOUT THE AUTHOR

I was born and raised in Lithuania. Since childhood, I've been very interested in biology. Why? Because it's the only subject where multiplication is the same thing as division (got the joke?). Simple as that.

In 9th grade, I started preparing for the biology olympiad, and in the next three years I won three golds in the Regional Biology Olympiad and three golds in the National Lithuanian Biology Olympiad (LitBO). I was then selected to represent Lithuania twice internationally, first in the 2012 IBO in Singapore and then in the 2013 IBO in Switzerland. I was awarded a bronze at each of these contests.

I then enrolled at a local medical school in my hometown, where I spent one year being humiliated and disrespected by the university staff. Being an incurable risk-taker, I left the medical school and transferred to a BSc Biomedical Sciences (Anatomy) degree at the University of Aberdeen in the United Kingdom. You're probably wondering why I didn't continue doing medicine or choose to do a PhD and go into research. In fact, for three years during my undergraduate studies I worked in the hospital, but after seeing the bureaucratic burden that doctors have to carry, I decided not to do medicine. For research, I did many summer projects (I'm super greedy for knowledge so I always did two internships over the summers): in 2015, I worked at the Institute of Medical Sciences in Aberdeen and then went to the Weizmann institute in Israel. In 2016, I got a scholarship to carry out an audit in the NHS Grampian Insulin Pump Clinic in Scotland and then went for two months to École Polytechnique Fédérale De Lausanne (Switzerland). I soon realized that the repetitive and monotonous lab environment didn't attract me, so anything that had to do with research (e.g., a PhD degree) wasn't an option anymore. In 2017, I was awarded a 1st class Bachelor's degree.

Printed in Great Britain
by Amazon